Name_____

Registered
Holy Fire® III Karuna Reiki® Master
Training Manual
Online and In-Person

William Lee Rand
The International Center for Reiki Training

9/29/20

Registered Holy Fire® III Karuna Reiki® Master Training Manual

Online and In-Person

First Edition, Spring, 1995
Second Edition, Summer, 1996
Third Edition, Late-Summer, 1996
Fourth Edition, Fall, 1996
Fifth Edition, Spring, 1998
Sixth Edition, Summer, 2001
Seventh Edition, Fall, 2007
Holy Fire® Edition, Spring, 2015
Holy Fire® II Edition, Winter, 2015
Format and Text Revision, June, 2016
Holy Fire® III Edition, June, 2019
Online Holy Fire® III Edition, June, 2020

ISBN: 1-886785-99-6

The International Center for Reiki Training
21421 Hilltop St., #28, Southfield, MI 48033 USA
Phone (800) 332-8112, (248) 948-8112, Fax (248) 948-9534
Email: center@reiki.org, Website: www.reiki.org

Holy Fire® and Karuna Reiki® are
registered service marks of William Lee Rand.

© Copyright, William L. Rand, 1995 - 2020

Making copies of any part of this manual is illegal unless permission is received from the Center. Please note that this material is sacred and is intended only for the personal use of those who have taken this training. These manuals are available for purchase by Karuna Reiki® teachers who have taken Karuna Reiki® training from a Registered Karuna Reiki® Master and have registered with the Center.

Notice

The Holy Fire® III Karuna Reiki® program is taught only by those who are registered with The International Center for Reiki Training. A registered teacher will have a certificate issued by their teacher. They will also provide a copy of this manual to each student and a certificate, and also have agreed to abide by a code-of-ethics and to use the Center teaching standards. Please see page 101-102 or contact the Center if you have questions.

*Your compassionate actions, as pure as gold,
will come back to you a thousand fold.*

The Logo

The Japanese kanji in the center of the logo means Reiki, which is spiritually guided life energy. The upward-pointing triangle represents humanity moving toward God. The downward-pointing triangle represents God moving toward humanity. Because the two triangles are united and balanced, they represent humanity and God working together in harmony. The inner sixteen-petaled flower symbolizes the throat chakra or communication. The outer twelve-petaled flower symbolizes the heart chakra or love. The complete logo represents Reiki, uniting God and humanity in harmony through the communication of love.

The Logo is the Registered Service Mark of The International Center for Reiki Training.

Holy Fire® and Karuna Reiki® Trademark Information

The words Holy Fire® and Karuna Reiki® are registered trademarks and require that the trademark symbol be used with them any time they are used—website, advertising, class materials, brochures, etc.

It is important to understand that it is not the energy that is trademarked but our system of Reiki that we use in our classes. The trademark for Holy Fire® applies to our work with Reiki only, maintaining the integrity of the energy and what we teach in our classes.

Note that the ® symbol can be found in the symbol section of most word processing programs. Here are the guidelines on how to use them properly:

Usui/Holy Fire® Reiki
(Then include either sentence below at the bottom of the page.)
® *Holy Fire is the registered service mark of William Lee Rand.*
OR
Holy Fire® is the registered service mark of William Lee Rand.
(In some instances, it may not be appropriate to use either
statement at the bottom of the page, i.e., certificates, business cards.)

Holy Fire® Karuna Reiki®
(Then include either sentence below at the bottom of the page.)
® *Holy Fire and Karuna Reiki are registered service marks of William Lee Rand.*
OR
Holy Fire® and Karuna Reiki® are registered service marks of William Lee Rand.
(In some instances, it may not be appropriate to use either
statement at the bottom of the page, i.e., certificates, business cards.)

Class Titles
Usui/Holy Fire® III Reiki I/II Training
Usui/Holy Fire® III Reiki Master Training
Holy Fire® III Karuna Reiki® Master Training

Table of Contents

The Logo v
Holy Fire® and Karuna Reiki® Trademark Information v
The Center Purpose and Philosophy ix

Holy Fire® III Karuna Reiki® Master Training Online

Introduction.. O-2
Online Reiki Class Outlines................................. O-7
Online Reiki Techniques O-20
Online Experiences and Ignitions......................... O-23
Holy Fire® Online Ignitions O-25
Online Teaching Best Practices O-27
Teacher and Student Online Preparations O-29
Sample Emails to Students................................. O-33
Online Teaching Tips O-37
Online Technology Recommendations O-38
Ship from Home O-40
Questions and Answers O-41

Registered Holy Fire® III Karuna Reiki® Master Training Manual In-Person

Holy Fire® III Karuna Reiki®................................ 10
Holy Fire, a New Reiki Energy 11
Healing Religious Trauma................................... 16
Birth of Holy Fire® II 19
Introduction to Holy Fire® III Reiki 20
The Twelve Heavens 27
The Formless Realm 31
The Brothers and Sisters of the Light..................... 32
Holy Fire® III Karuna Reiki® Symbols 35
Karuna Reiki® I Symbols 37
    Zonar 37
    Halu 39
    Harth 41
    Rama 43

- Karuna Reiki® II Symbols 45
  - Gnosa 45
  - Iava 46
  - Shanti 47
  - Kriya 48
- Holy Fire® Symbol 49
- Holy Fire® Meditation 51
- Soul and Spirit Defined 52
- Growing in the Experience 53
- Healing Spirit Attachments 53
- Experiences, Placements and Ignitions Explained 57
- Unique Format for Experiences, Placements and Ignitions .. 58
- Ocean of Holy Love Experience 58
- Holy Love Experience 61
- Heavenly Banquet Hall Experience 64
- Holy Fire® Healing Experience Explained 65
- Preparations for a Holy Fire® III Healing Experience 66
- Holy Fire® Healing Experience 67
- Empowered by the River of Life Experience 69
- Holy Fire® Placements Reiki I & II, Master Practitioner .. 71
- Master Ignitions 73
- Understanding Your Ignition Experience 76
- Teaching Holy Fire® III Karuna Reiki® Classes 77
- Receiving Ignitions by Yourself 77
- Holy Fire® III Reiki and Spiritual Guidance 77
- Maintain and Develop Your Holy Fire® Energy 79
- Holy Fire® III Class Outlines 80
  - Usui/Holy Fire® III Reiki I Training 81
  - Usui/Holy Fire® III Reiki II Training 82
  - Usui/Holy Fire® III Reiki Master 83
  - Usui/Holy Fire® III Reiki Master Class 85
  - Holy Fire® III Karuna Reiki® Master Class 87
  - Holy Fire® III Upgrade Class 91
  - Giving a Holy Fire® Reiki Talk 92
- Chanting & Toning with Holy Fire® III Karuna Reiki® 95
  - Chanting with Holy Fire® III Karuna Reiki® 96
  - Toning with Holy Fire® III Karuna Reiki® 97

RMA Code of Ethics 99
RMA Standards of Practice 100
Minimum Teaching Requirements 101
The Promise of a Thriving Reiki Practice 102
Create a Thriving Reiki Practice, Part I 103
Create a Thriving Reiki Practice, Part II 110
World Peace 119

Forms and Resources
Reiki Symbol Test 133
Reiki Client Information Form 135
Reiki Documentation Form 137
Holy Fire® III Karuna Reiki® Class Evaluation Form 138
Anatomy for Reiki 140
About the International Center for Reiki Training 142
Purchasing Holy Fire® III Karuna Reiki® Manuals 143

Differences Between Holy Fire® II and Holy Fire® III
The main changes are the addition of a Holy Love IV Experience, the elimination of a pre-Ignition, and the use of four Ignitions instead of three.

The Center's Purpose

- To establish and maintain standards for teaching Reiki.
- To train practitioners and teachers.
- To create instruction manuals for use in Reiki classes.
- To encourage the establishment of Reiki support groups where people can give and receive Reiki sessions.
- To encourage students to become successful Reiki teachers if they are guided to do so.
- To research new information about Reiki and to develop new techniques to improve its use.
- To openly acknowledge the value provided by all Reiki practitioners and teachers regardless of their lineage or affiliation.
- To promote friendly cooperation between all Reiki practitioners and teachers toward the goal of healing ourselves and planet Earth through the use of Reiki.

The Center's Philosophy

- Honesty and clarity in one's thinking.
- The willingness to recognize prejudice in one's self and replace it with truth and love. Have compassion for those who have decided not to do this.
- Speaking the truth without judgment or blame.
- Respect for the right of others to form their own values and beliefs.
- Placing greater value on learning from experience and inner guidance than on the teachings of an authority.
- Basing the value of a theory or technique on the verifiable results it helps one achieve.
- Being open to results rather than attached to them.
- Taking personal responsibility for one's situation in life.
- Assuming that one has the resources to resolve any problem encountered, or the ability to develop those resources.
- Using negative and positive experiences to heal and grow.
- Trusting completely in the Higher Power regardless of the name one chooses to call it.
- The complete expression of Love as the highest goal.

Holy Fire® III Karuna Reiki® Master Training
Online

Use the information in this section, including the class outlines, to teach online classes and also read the whole manual as all the material is part of the class. If you are teaching or taking the class in person, read the whole manual, but teach using the class outlines beginning on page 80.

Introduction

At the ICRT, we believe it is our responsibility to provide a stable source of consistent, high-quality Reiki training based on an accurate history and a well-organized presentation. This concept is what we have adhered to for over thirty years in teaching our own classes as well as training others to be successful Reiki students and teachers. The basis for our success is carefully listening to and following the guidance that the wisdom of Reiki provides to us. And at the same time, keeping our finger on the pulse of current events taking place in the world so we can provide solutions to problems as they come up, modifying our teaching methods to deal with changing circumstances in society. Our online teaching course fulfills these needs. Students agree that it is a superior training system in both its organization and in the quality of the Reiki energy it provides.

The Challenges of Changing Times
The coronavirus posed severe problems worldwide when the December 2019 outbreak in China rapidly spread to the United States. By the end of March 2020, with no antiviral drug or vaccine for COVID-19 available, authorities recommended staying at home to avoid infection or to avoid spreading infection if one is an unknown carrier. In some areas, this became a requirement, while in others, travel outside the home was permissible only to get food or medical help or conduct other indispensable tasks. For anyone working outside the home, going to work became an impossibility. With a record number of layoffs, an ever-growing number of people experienced a complex set of problems, avoiding infection while creating alternate ways to earn a living.

With the changing conditions, Reiki people experienced restrictions for giving in-person Reiki to others, unless part of the same household. These restrictions also prevented people from teaching Reiki classes. Such circumstances limit the practice of Reiki and restrict the number of Reiki practitioners to those already trained. Reiki Masters, who taught part or full time, found they could not derive an income from teaching classes, critical when so many were out of work. Two developments brought us a solution to these circumstances. We received a method for online Reiki training, and with it, a higher quality of Reiki energy that integrates our spiritual awareness with the technology of the internet to adapt to the swiftly changing world.

A New Reiki Frequency
Motivated by a desire to help, William Rand prayed and sought spiritual guidance. Also, our global community of Reiki people used the World Peace Grid as a powerful force to connect and unify us with a common purpose. The intention and prayer of the grid inscription, "May the followers of all religions and spiritual paths, work together to create peace among all people on Earth," created worldwide unity. (Note: See "World Peace," *Holy Fire® III Reiki Master Manual,* p. 151.) During our time of need, the divine realms heard and listened to our collective vision and prayer through the power of Reiki energy.

Enlightened beings, who call themselves the Brothers and the Sisters of the Light, also known as the Ascended Masters, answered our prayers. While living on the Earth, these beings founded all the world's religions and spiritual paths, which for the most part, contain separate practices. In the higher heavenly realms, united as one and hearing our prayers, they guided us to discover and recognize the spiritual energy needed to help ourselves and others. Responding to our needs, they sent a new frequency of Reiki to the people of Earth.

On March 20, 2020, during the spring equinox and a session with Colleen Benelli, William and Colleen received a unique Ignition, which enabled them to give Placements and Ignitions at a distance and teach distant Reiki classes. Also, the Reiki energy's strength and quality increased, allowing them to pass this new ability on to others through distant Reiki classes. Previously, the only online class William taught was the January 2019 Holy Fire® III Reiki Upgrade webinar. This capability was possible because he received a series of individual Ignitions from Jesus, who was also energetically present during the webinar.

Throughout the history of Reiki, we can observe how Reiki energy is continually developed. Usui Sensei's first decision when he received Reiki was to spread Reiki to all the world. To quicken the pace of this development, he said the most important quality for a Reiki Master to have is continually seeking to develop the quality and quantity of Reiki energy one can channel. Usui Sensei, Hayashi Sensei, and Takata Sensei felt guided to adapt and develop Reiki according to the peoples' needs. Similarly, we received an extraordinary new Reiki light to lift us, guide, and empower us to enter a state of unification more easily on Earth.

During the coronavirus crisis, the Brothers and Sisters of the Light, who brought us Holy Fire® Reiki, guided the introduction of online Reiki classes. This method enables Holy Fire® Reiki teachers to conduct classes using a new Online Ignition system, ensuring an increase in the number of practitioners and teachers. We also received a significant improvement in Reiki's quality, as this version of Holy Fire® Reiki is a more powerful and effective healing energy. By combining this divine gift with human capabilities, we began providing real-world solutions for the Reiki community. We offered a way to continue teaching Reiki classes and cope with the limitations presented by the coronavirus pandemic. We were grateful for receiving this gift at such a crucial time.

The Role of Technological Development
As part of this process, we acknowledge the vital role of technological development in teaching the online Reiki system. As we began the journey, we knew spiritual beings guided the introduction of technology to humanity. They intend us to be aware of them. Through this awareness, they help people use technology with greater clarity and mastery.

As we worked with them, they helped us harmonize the use of technology with Reiki energy development. Our knowledge has kept up with our needs, as working with others over the internet is more manageable. We are now providing high-quality live Reiki training to others anywhere in the world. It is at a level where you can easily sense the teacher's presence, other students, and the love and caring of the Reiki energy.

An Innovative System for Online Classes
On April 4, 2020, William Rand and Colleen Benelli taught a webinar in which participants received the Holy Fire® Online Ignition and learned how to teach online classes. The webinar is available as a recording for you to take part in to upgrade your Holy Fire® Reiki energy, and it gives you the ability to teach online classes. It will enable you to continue teaching your Reiki classes online from your home. The same Ignition will also allow you to teach classes in person when it is safe to do so.

The Holy Fire® healing system is one in which the energy has been continuously working to help students evolve to higher levels of consciousness since its inception in 2014. This evolution makes it possible to teach online classes. And since the beginning of Holy Fire® III, the energy has been working with each student's energy field to prepare them for this next phase. It is fortuitous we were ready for this development when we needed to cope with the issues brought on by the coronavirus.

When new healing energy manifests, it is usually important to take the time to gain experience and develop a deeper understanding of its nature and how to use it before sharing it with others. However, the Brothers and Sisters of the Light knew in advance about the need for this new energy. They were working with us and all Holy Fire® students to develop our energy so each would be ready to accept the Online Ignition energy when needed.

This new energy looks and feels impressive and heals by making it easier for students to become their Authentic Self. During the process, the Brothers and Sisters of the Light counsel the parts that need healing. In these sessions, the parts can express all their concerns, and as they do this, they become healed. This healing occurs in the person's background awareness on one of the higher heavens, as the individual focuses on the Authentic Self. Revealing the Authentic Self generates healing. It is a pathway of unification in which one's self-image merges with the Authentic Self and is the pathway of empowerment.

This innovative system allows us to continue teaching during changing times. Classes are live instruction in a video-webinar format in real-time, not a recording. The teacher communicates with each student during class, interacting, and answering questions. Students interact with each other to share Reiki and exchange ideas. We use air hugs to hug each other over the video call. This practice is an example of Reiki responding to societal changes lovingly to continue to bless us.

There is a greater emphasis on self-Reiki and distance Reiki in this system. It provides online Placements and Ignitions that enable you to give them to your students when teaching online classes. Current technology allows you to teach relatively large classes; we encourage you to teach smaller classes if a larger number does not feel right. And in fact, we recommend you teach about the same number of students you usually teach. By doing this, the class will be small enough for the students to have their questions answered and receive the attention they require for your classes to go well.

Digital Manuals
The online teaching system uses the Holy Fire® Reiki method of teaching, providing class outlines for all Reiki classes, including Reiki Master and Karuna Master. To aid in teaching online classes, we provide digital versions of our training manuals. We recommend each student receive a manual before class. The digital version is online viewing only; downloading and printing are not available. Teachers and students can read digital versions on a smartphone, tablet, or computer. Students will receive access to their digital class manual after they sign up for a class, so there is no concern over how long it will take for a class manual to arrive. Digital manuals go well with online teaching. Your students can be anywhere in the country or the world and get their class manual immediately.

Digital manuals are available for purchase on our website (www.reiki.org/digital). Teachers can purchase up to five digital manuals of the same class manual on one order to send to separate students, and receive the full bulk discounts. You can purchase more manuals for each class by placing additional orders of up to five. Purchase digital products like any other item. Once your purchase is complete, go to your profile page and click on the Digital Documents tab to view your digital manuals. If you are buying manuals for students, you will need to ensure each student has an account in our system. Be sure you have the email address associated with each student's account. Once you notify them of their manual, students access them in the same way, logging into their account and clicking on the Digital Documents tab.

The hard copy manuals will continue to be available and will contain the online teaching section as well as the in-person outlines located in the middle of the manual.

Teaching Online versus In-Person Instruction
Advances in technology now provide us with the ability to give quality, live Reiki training online in real-time. Video conferencing empowers us to teach a professional level of Reiki where our students receive excellent training and the extraordinary Holy Fire® Online Reiki energy. There are some differences in teaching Reiki online versus in person.

The Holy Fire® Online Reiki class training includes new online distant Reiki techniques. Both digital Master manuals begin with a Master Training Online Training section. This section contains details for both the teacher and student: the Holy Fire® online Reiki outlines, online Reiki teaching techniques, online

Experiences and Ignitions, best online practices, and preparations and teaching tips, and online technology recommendations for both the online Reiki class teacher and student. In addition, the online Ignitions gives one the ability to teach Reiki classes both online and in-person when it becomes safe to do so.

We spend additional class time doing self-Reiki and distant Reiki practice. Students also learn how to give Reiki sessions online, including Byosen scanning and all the hand positions. There is a new symbol practice technique, a distant Gyoshi-ho practice, and the new level of Reiki energy seems to make everything flow smoothly.

We intend to spread Reiki in the world today in every way possible. We encourage Reiki teachers to teach other teachers who can teach more teachers to teach the students. This information, and the support and love from Reiki, provide you with the skill and confidence to teach your online Reiki classes with the same love and personal warmth as your in-person classes.

While we all enjoy classes where we can meet in person, there are new options. If circumstances require that we practice social distancing, we can now be socially connected as we expand our skills to include both online and in-person classes.

Whether we are aware of it, each of us is in our current life situation for the long haul. And as we rise to any challenge, we are called upon to share our gifts, express our love, and follow our inner guidance. By doing this, even if we are practicing social distancing, we draw closer together in our hearts.

Online Reiki Class Outlines

The following class outlines are made available for your use. These are the class outlines used by the members of the Reiki Membership Association and by our Licensed Reiki Master Teachers when teaching online. The outlines combine the Western-style of Reiki with the Japanese style and Holy Fire® III Reiki style when teaching online classes.

The Reiki I & II outlines are made to be used with *Reiki, The Healing Touch, First and Second Degree Manual* class manual along with the Online section, which includes instructions on how to do all the techniques in the Online outlines, including the Japanese Reiki Techniques (JRT). You may also want to get a copy of the *Japanese Reiki Techniques Workshop DVD*, instructing you on practicing all the Japanese Reiki Techniques. Consider ordering one and notifying your students to get this DVD, available at www.reiki.org/store/cds-and-dvds.

The Reiki Master Online class outlines are to be used with the hard copy manual. These Online Reiki class outlines are downloadable from our website. Mail each student a hard copy of the class manual when they sign up and include a copy of the symbols, if symbols are part of the class, for memorizing them. Explain the private nature of the symbols and that they should not share them with others. You could also include information about how they may want to buy a practice dummy from Amazon.com.

Students who attend the Online Reiki classes will be able to practice and teach Reiki both online and in person.

Changes in the Reiki I & II Outlines for Online Reiki I & II
Online Reiki I & II classes include Reiki techniques for giving Reiki sessions at a distance and in person. Also, there are some changes in how we teach the online, versus the in-person outlines to accommodate virtual training. For example, in Reiki I, self-Reiki is taught, and in Reiki II, the student learns how to provide Reiki sessions for others in person and at a distance.

Reiki I Online Outline
1. Only Self-Reiki is taught, #16 (versus the in-person outline #16, where we explain and practice the standard treatment for treating others with all hand positions).
2. Reiki symbol discussion is taught, #19 (versus the in-person outline, which explains it in Reiki II, #3).

Reiki II Online Outline
1. Placement for Level II empowering the symbols is given in the morning, #7 (versus the in-person outline, where we give it in the afternoon, #7).
2. Hand Positions for treating others is now taught and practiced in Reiki II, #12 (versus the in-person outline for Reiki I, where we practice in #16).

Usui/Holy Fire® III
Online Reiki I Training

Suggested class time: 9:00 A.M.–6:30 P.M.

Reiki I can be taught by itself or as part of a combined Reiki I&II class. If it is combined, send each student a copy of the Reiki II symbols when they sign-up and let them know they must memorize them for a test that will be given in class.

1. Acknowledge and welcome each student as they arrive online.
2. Explain the Zoom technology used in class: mute, unmute, chat, and online etiquette.
3. Explain and demonstrate the Kenyoku technique and have the students practice (*Reiki: The Healing Touch*, p. 61). Have students their raise hands, and place positive energy all over their room. They then look at each person separately on the screen and give each an air hug (p. O-22).
4. Introductions: name, location, why you decided to take this class, and something you like about yourself. As each person introduces themselves, check them off on the class roster. The teacher introduces themselves last.
5. *Ocean of Holy Love Experience* (*Master Manual*, p. 78). Explain how the Experience process works and that you will provide a brief guided meditation, then stop talking while they play the class music in the background and receive energy directly from the Holy Fire®. Have students write about their experiences and share them.
6. Main Reiki Talk. Explain the meaning of Rei and ki, the different levels of Reiki, how Reiki works, and how the Placement process works, what Reiki can be used for. (Use examples and Reiki stories to explain these topics.) Explain the history: Usui, Hayashi, Takata and the 22 Masters; include information on the Gakkai and the discovery of the Japanese Reiki Techniques; the *Hayashi Healing Guide* as part of history and a brief history of Holy Fire® Reiki, including Online Reiki.
7. Explain and review *The Original Reiki Ideals*. Explain that we use the Online Holy Fire® III Reiki energy in class and that the techniques come from traditional Usui Reiki.
8. Lunch (one hour).
9. Return and regroup and share air hugs with all students.
10. Explain Gassho meditation (*Reiki: The Healing Touch*, p. 56).
11. Briefly explain the Twelve Heavens concept. Give details about the first three (*Master Manual*, pp. 54-55), and talk about the Online Placement and how it works.
12. Reiki I Online Placement.
13. Ask students to write about their Placement experience and then share.
14. Break (10 minutes).
15. Byosen self-scanning. Demonstrate and explain Byosen self-scanning. Explain that in the same way the Placement opens their palm chakras to channel Reiki, it also opens them to detect where a person needs Reiki. Then guide students to practice Byosen on themselves, finding a few places that need Reiki and then

treating them. Explain that Byosen is also used when treating others. (*Healing Touch*, pp. 55-58). Explain Reiji-ho (*Healing Touch*, p. 54) and that it is more advanced as one uses intuition rather than hand sensitivity.

16. Explain that it is important to give oneself a Reiki session each day. Then guide the class through a self-Reiki session: Refer to each hand position in the manual and use a stopwatch. Determine the amount of time for each position based on the amount of time you have left in class. Use all the positions through 13b. Have students use the Kenyoku technique at the end of the practice session.
17. Take a 10-minute break.
18. Ask the students to share about their experience with self-Reiki and ask if they have questions.
19. Give a brief talk on the Reiki II symbols and explain they are part of Reiki II. If this is a combined Reiki I&II class, remind the students they need to memorize the symbols for a test the next day.
20. Closing meditation or prayer.

Usui/Holy Fire® III
Online Reiki II Training
Suggested class time: 9:00 A.M.–6:30 P.M.

Reiki I&II can be taught separately or together as a two to three-day class. Send each student a copy of the Reiki II symbols by email/attached file as soon as they sign up for class. Explain that they need to memorize each of the symbols for class and that there will be a test on the symbols in class.

1. Acknowledge and welcome each student as they arrive online and check them off on the class roster.
2. Explain the Zoom technology used in class: mute, unmute, chat, and online etiquette.
3. Demonstrate the *Energy Clearing Technique* (p. O-22). Explain that you will be sending them into breakout rooms, with two to each room, where they will introduce themselves, then take turns giving each other *Energy Clearing*. Then get air hugs (p. O-22).
4. If this is a separate Reiki II class, then use #3 from the Reiki I outline. Otherwise, if this is part of a Reiki I & II class, have the students say good morning and greet each other. Then have each student place Reiki all over their room and get air hugs from everyone while playing the Nomad *River Crossing* music.
5. *Holy Love Experience*. Have students write their experiences in their notebooks and share them.
6. Explain each of the three Reiki II symbols. Show how to draw them and describe what each is for and how to use them.
7. Lunch (one hour). Students can use some of their lunchtimes to memorize the symbols.
8. Talk on Reiki II symbols. Provide a complete understanding, including the history of each symbol, what each is for, and how to draw and use them.

Include the many ways to use the Distant symbol for past, present, and future healing. Explain why they need to be kept private (*Healing Touch*, p. 45), and that the symbols and teaching system comes from Usui Reiki Ryoho, and the energy for each symbol comes from Holy Fire® Reiki.

9. Test on symbols. Have the students draw the three symbols on paper with their books closed and place their name on their paper. Call each student by name and ask the student to hold their completed test up to the camera so the teacher can verify their test. If there are errors, gently point them out and ask the student to correct them. Use hints if necessary, or have the student use their notes. Coach, so everyone passes.
10. Explain the Reiki II Placement. Conduct the Reiki II Placement (*Master Manual*, p. 92). Ask the students to play the Julie True, *Music to Journal By, Vol. One, Healing Presence* music.
11. Have students write their Placement experiences in their notebooks and share.
12. Air hugs (p. O-22).
13. Break (10 minutes).
14. Review and practice the hand positions for treating others as described in *Reiki, The Healing Touch,* page 83, and explain how to do a complete session using all the symbols.
    a. Explain to the students that they will be placed in a breakout room to meet their partner before they take turns practicing the hand positions using the Distant symbol.
    b. Send students into the breakout rooms for a couple of minutes, where they will introduce themselves, write down each other's names, and decide who will receive first. Bring the students back to the main room.
    c. Each will need a doll or Teddy bear or dummy to represent their partner when they send Reiki. The teacher guides the senders in how to use HSZSN to give distant Reiki, or what is called Enkaku Chiryo in Japanese, to their partner. The student who is giving Reiki first will open their manual to Chapter 9 and use each of the hand positions listed in their manual, ending with position #11. Let them know the back positions are optional, depending on the needs of the client.
    d. Using a stopwatch, time and guide the sender through each of the hand positions, starting with Position 1, then Position 2, and so on. Base the time for each position on the time that is available. Usually, it will be 1.5 to 3 minutes per hand position.
    e. Ask the students to give some of the hand positions using no symbol and some using the Power symbol, or the Mental/Emotional symbol based on their own intuition or the needs of the client. Or they could do part of a position with no symbol and part of the same position using the Power symbol or the Mental/Emotional symbol to experience the effect of each of the symbols.
    f. When the first session is completed, have the students take notes on what was experienced.
    g. Break time, 5-10 minutes.
    h. The receiver becomes the sender, the sender becomes the receiver, and the above sequence is repeated.

i. When completed, the partners are placed back into their breakout rooms for ten minutes or so to share about their experience with each other.
  j. Bring all students to the main room and have those who volunteer share their experiences with the whole class.
15. Explain Gyoshi-ho and the exercise (*Healing Touch*, p. 62). While in the main room, and using the same partner used when the hand positions were practiced, have one receive by being relaxed and receptive with palms up and the other sending Gyoshi-ho to their partner using the eyes. The sender will focus only on the image of their partner while the whole class is on the main screen. Practice Gyoshi-ho. Explain that a practitioner can use this in a regular distance or in-person session (p. O-21). When done, send the students back into the breakout room with their partner to share what was experienced.
16. Point out the *Anatomy for Reiki* section, and explain the *Reiki Client Information Form*, *Reiki Documentation Form* (*Healing Touch*, pp. 148-149; and *Master Manual*, pp. 167-169) and charging money for Reiki sessions or bartering.
17. Go over the ICRT RMA *Code of Ethics* and *Standards of Practice* (*Healing Touch*, pp. 176-177 or *Master Manual*, p. 144-145).
18. Have students pick a Reiki Buddy to send distant Reiki to after class.
19. Ending meditation or prayer and group air hugs.
20. Have students complete their class reviews and email them to you before sending the students their class certificates.
21. Encourage students to participate in an online Reiki support group.

Usui/Holy Fire® III
Online Reiki Master Class

Suggested class time: 9:00 A.M.–6:30 P.M.
This outline is for teaching the 3-day Reiki Master class.

Day 1

1. Acknowledge each student as they arrive online and check them off on the class roster. Explain the Zoom technology used in class: mute, unmute, chat, and online etiquette.
2. Explain and demonstrate the Kenyoku technique and have the students practice (*Reiki, The Healing Touch*, p. 61). Students raise hands, place positive energy all over the room, and get air hugs from everyone. Look at each person separately on the screen and give them an air hug (p. O-22).
3. Introductions: name, where you are from, why you decided to take this class, and something you love about yourself. As each person introduces themself, check them off on the class roster.
4. Explain our definitions of Soul and Spirit (*Master Manual*, p. 27), and the Twelve Heavens (*Master Manual*, p. 54). Explain that the energy in this class is based on the Usui/Holy Fire® III system.
5. Explain the unique way Online Holy Fire® III Experiences, Placements and

Ignitions are performed, and that students will not learn how to give hands-on attunements in this class but will give the Placement style of attunements instead. Placements are for Reiki I and II and part of Master. They provide a stronger, more powerful healing energy for the student, open students to higher consciousness, and activate the symbol(s). Explain how Holy Fire® III works and the concepts of the Authentic Self, the Culturally Created Self, and the Dormant Self.

6. *Empowered by the River of Life Experience*. Introduction: use the Online section of the Master manual to explain the *River of Life Experience* (p. O-23). Explain this Experience will be healing and give students the ability to give online Placements for Reiki I and II, and it will also empower the Usui Master symbol in the Online Reiki Master class.
7. *Empowered by the River of Life Experience*: use the script in the Online section, page O-23, for the Experience. Ask students to write about it and share.
8. Explain the World Peace Grid, using crystals and stones with Reiki, and how to use a single crystal to send Reiki continuously. Discuss how making a Reiki grid using the World Peace Crystal Grid will continue to send Reiki to yourself and others: used for distant healing, personal healing, goals, and manifestation. Note: This step can be done later in the day, or if there is no time, on the second day.
9. The Usui Dai Ko Myo symbol: show it to the students, explain usage, practice drawing it. Go over the meaning of the Japanese words and explain what it means to Reiki people.
10. Show the Holy Fire® symbol. Explain its history, how to draw it, and talk about its four aspects: purification, healing, guidance, and empowerment.
11. Lunch (one hour). Use some of the lunchtime to memorize symbols.
12. Test on both symbols.
13. Explain how Online Placements work; they do not come from the teacher or through the teacher but come to the student directly from the Holy Fire®.
14. Master Practitioner Online Placement (*Master Manual*, p. 92). Students write about their experiences and share them.
15. Break.
16. Explain the Online Ignition process and that you will give a brief guided meditation and then stop talking while the energy guides the student directly. Explain that some students may have inner experiences, and some may only feel relaxed, and that the most important effects take place below the student's level of awareness. Explain that the four Online Ignitions holistically empower the Holy Fire® symbol in a unique way that is right for each student.
17. First Online Ignition (*Master Manual*, p. 94). Give students time to write about their experiences and share them.
18. *Symbol Practice Technique* (p. O-20). Explain that the Holy Fire® symbol has its own ability to send Reiki at a distance, and the HSZSN symbol is not needed. Divide students into breakout rooms of 2, 3 or 4 students. Have them write down the names of those in their group and decide the order in which each will receive; 1,2,3,4, etc. When they return to the main room, the teacher guides the students to practice giving the Dai Ko Myo and Holy Fire® energies to the

others in their group, using 5-10 minutes per symbol. The teacher times for each student and tells when to switch. Students share experiences in between each client, discussing how they experienced the energy of each symbol.
19. Break.
20. *Reiki Moving Meditation*. The teacher demos the meditation on camera for the students to see, and then the students follow the teacher. This exercise can be covered now or the second or third day, and if the next day, use the Holy Fire® symbol rather than the DKM (*Master Manual*, p. 24).

Day 2

1. Acknowledge each student as they arrive online and check them off on the class roster.
2. Demonstrate the *Reiki Energy Clearing Technique* (p. O-22). Divide students into breakout rooms with two students per room, and practice on each other. Place Reiki all over the room and get air hugs.
3. Second Online Ignition (*Master Manual*, p. 94). Give students time to write about their experiences and share them.
4. Explain the evolution of Reiki and how it developed from Usui Reiki into Holy Fire® Reiki and then to Online Reiki.
5. Describe the history of Holy Fire® Reiki.
6. Describe the essence of Reiki.
7. Explain Holy Fire® III Reiki and spiritual guidance.
8. Lunch (one hour).
9. Third Online Ignition. Follow instructions in the Online section (p. O-26). Have students write experiences in notebooks, then share.
10. Review Distant Reiki from *Reiki, The Healing Touch*, page 50.
11. Practice giving Distant Reiki sessions in breakout rooms using Holy Fire® Reiki. Two to four students in one breakout room, giving Reiki to one per room.
12. Break for 10 to 15 minutes.
13. *Holy Fire® Healing Experience*, as described in the *Usui/Holy Fire® III Reiki Master Manual*, pages 85-87.
    - Explain the Holy Fire® Healing Experience.
    - Guide the students through the preparations.
    - Have the students choose one thing they would like healed or a goal to empower.
    - Make sure everyone has completed the description of their issue.
    - Conduct the *Holy Fire® Healing Experience* using the script on page 87.
    - Have students share their experiences.
14. If there is extra time, you could do one of the *Holy Love Experiences*.
15. Questions and Answers.

Day 3

1. Acknowledge each student as they arrive online and check them off on the class roster.
2. Demonstrate the *Reiki Energy Clearing Technique* (p. O-22). Divide students

into breakout rooms with two students per room, and practice on each other. Place Reiki all over the room and get air hugs.

3. Fourth Online Ignition. Follow Online Ignition instructions (p. O-26). Have students write their experiences in their notebooks, then share.
4. Discussion of the values and spiritual orientation of a true Reiki Master, *Values That Bring Success on All Levels* (Master Manual, p. 146).
5. Questions and Answers, or discuss other Holy Fire® concepts.
6. Lunch (one hour).
7. Practice giving Distant Reiki sessions in breakout rooms using Holy Fire®. Use the same method as in Day 1, #18. Have students compare their experience with the first time they shared Holy Fire® energy on Day 1.
8. Explain how to practice the *Holy Fire® Meditation* (Master Manual, p. 26). Practice it if there is time.
9. Explain healing religious trauma (Master Manual, p. 43).
10. Explain *The Brothers and Sisters of the Light, Unification Consciousness, Becoming the Authentic Self,* and *The Spirit of the Earth* (Master Manual, pp. 58-60).
11. Explain *Healing Spirit Attachments* and conduct this process for the class (Master Manual, p. 28).
12. Explain the Experiences, Placements and Ignitions; how these are done, and go over the scripts. Practicing is usually not needed.
13. Conduct another of the *Holy Love Experiences* if there is time.
14. Talk about online teaching, go over class Online Outlines, and suggest students take the ICRT Online Reiki training webinar entitled *Holy Fire® Online Reiki Master Training Recording*.
15. Explain *Receiving Ignitions by Yourself* (Master Manual, 97).
16. Go over the *Code of Ethics* and *Standards of Practice* for online and in-person sessions.
17. Talk about developing your Reiki practice and the value of membership in the Reiki Membership Association (RMA).
18. Have students complete their class review and email it to the teacher.
19. Closing prayer.

Holy Fire® III Online Karuna Reiki® Master Class Outline
Suggested class time: 9:00 A.M.–6:30 P.M.
This outline is for teaching the 3-day Karuna Reiki® Master class.

Day 1
1. Acknowledge each student as they arrive online and check them off on the class roster.
2. Explain the Zoom technology used in class: mute, unmute, chat, and online etiquette.
3. Explain and demonstrate the Kenyoku technique and have the students practice (*Reiki, The Healing Touch*, p. 61). Have students raise hands, place positive energy all over their room, and get air hugs from everyone. Look at each person separately on the screen and give them an air hug (p. O-22).

4. Introductions: name, where are you from, why you decided to take this class, and something you love about yourself. As each person introduces themself, check them off on the class roster.
5. Explain our definitions of Soul and Spirit (*Karuna Manual*, p. 52), the Twelve Heavens (*Karuna Manual*, p. 27), and letting go of guides. Explain that the energy in this class is based on the Usui/Holy Fire® III system.
6. Explain the unique way Online Holy Fire® III Experiences, Placements and Ignitions are performed, and that in this class, four Online Ignitions are given. The four Online Ignitions activate the nine symbols and give the student the ability to give online and in-person Placements and Ignitions. Also, explain that after this class, the teacher can teach both in-person and online classes and give the Placement style of attunement when teaching Reiki I and II and when activating the Usui Master symbol in the Reiki Master class. The Placement and Ignition attunements are easier to do and provide a stronger and more effective experience.
7. Explain the concepts of the Authentic Self, the Culturally Created Self, and the Dormant Self.
8. *Empowered by the River of Life Experience*. Introduction: use the introduction script in the Online section, page O-23. Explain that this Experience will be healing and give students the ability to give online Placements for Reiki I & II, and it will also empower the Usui Master symbol in the Online Reiki Master class.
9. *Empowered by the River of Life Experience*: use the script in the Online section, page O-23. Have students write about their experiences and share them.
10. Break.
11. Give a brief history of Reiki, including the idea that Reiki has evolved with Usui, Hayashi, and Takata. There is no limit to the quantity and quality of Reiki possible for us to channel. Explain the development of online Reiki classes.
12. Explain Holy Fire® III Karuna Reiki®, including origin. Explain Holy Fire® III Reiki and spiritual guidance (*Karuna Manual*, p. 10).
13. Lunch.
14. Explain that the class is both a practitioner and a master class. Explain that the Master Ignitions initiate the student as a Karuna Reiki® Master, with the ability to teach and give Ignitions. It also attunes the student to each of the eight practitioner symbols for use in sessions.
15. Explain how students can teach all their classes as Holy Fire® classes, including Reiki I and II, Usui/Holy Fire® Reiki Master, and Karuna Reiki® Master. The Holy Fire® Placements for Usui/Holy Fire® I and II and Master will be explained in class.
16. Discuss how Ignitions work and that Ignitions are attunements. Explain how you will give a brief guided meditation and then stop talking while the energy guides the student directly. Explain that some students may have inner experiences, and some may just feel relaxed. The most important effects take place below the student's level of awareness. Explain that the four Online Ignitions holistically empower all nine Karuna symbols, and this process works uniquely for each student.
17. Do the first Online Ignition with integration time and sharing (*Karuna Manual*, p. 74).
18. Break.

19. Talk about each of the Karuna I symbols and the Holy Fire® symbol, how to draw them, and what they are used for and go over them thoroughly.
20. Test on the Holy Fire® symbol and the Karuna I symbols.
21. Break.
22. Talk about the Karuna II symbols, how to draw them, and what they are used for and go over them thoroughly.
23. Test on the Karuna II symbols. An alternate method is to teach all nine symbols simultaneously and give one test for all of them.
24. Ending prayer or affirmation. Air hugs.

Day 2

1. Acknowledge each student as they arrive online and check them off on the class roster.
2. Explain Zoom breakout rooms.
3. Demonstrate the Reiki *Energy Clearing Technique* (p. O-22). Divide students into breakout rooms with two students per room and practice on each other. Place Reiki all over the room and get air hugs.
4. Ask students to share how they are experiencing the class and any questions or comments.
5. Second Online Ignition (*Karuna Manual*, p. 74).
6. Break.
7. Talk about the trademark for Holy Fire® III Karuna Reiki® and why it was developed. Let them know we include the certificate for this class when they purchase the manual. Go over the registration process and how it works.
8. Lunch.
9. Third Online Ignition. Follow instructions in the Online section (p. O-26). Have students write experiences in notebooks, then share.
10. Break.
11. *Symbol Practice Technique* (p. O-20). Divide students into breakout rooms of 2, 3 or 4 students. Have them write down the names of those in their breakout room and decide the order in which each will receive Reiki with each getting a number – 1,2,3 etc. Return to the main room. Explain that the Holy Fire® symbol gives them the ability to send Reiki at a distance. Have them practice giving the Holy Fire® symbol, and each of the first four Karuna Reiki symbols' energies, to each other in sessions. Use 5-10 minutes per symbol. All the students in each group give Reiki to one. Have them share, discussing how they experienced each symbol's energy.
12. Explain Experiences, Placements and Ignitions, how these are done, and go over the scripts. Practicing is usually not needed.
13. Explain how to practice the *Holy Fire® Meditation* (*Karuna Manual*, p 51). Practice it if you have time.
14. End class with prayer, affirmation, or air hugs.

Day 3

1. Acknowledge each student as they arrive online, check them off on the class roster.
2. Demonstrate the *Reiki Energy Clearing Technique* (p. O-22). Divide students into

breakout rooms with two students per room and practice on each other. Place Reiki all over the room, get air hugs. Have them return to the main room when done.

3. Ask students to share how they are experiencing the class and if there are any questions or comments.
4. Fourth Online Ignition. Follow Online Ignition instructions (p. O-26). Have students write experiences in notebooks, then share them.
5. Go over the Online Outlines for all levels. Discuss how teachers need to keep their energy out of the Experiences, Placements and Ignitions; how these are done without the teacher physically interacting with students. The teacher does not hold space or intend but focuses on keeping their energy back from the students and held close to the teacher's body. Explain that this allows the energies to go straight to the student without being slowed or affected by the teacher, keeping the energy pure, powerful, and effective. However, the teacher can pray directly to God, Source, Creator, and so forth, praying for the students' benefit and asking that God's will for each student be fully manifested.
6. Cover any additional topics, such as the World Peace Reiki Grid project or the benefits of the RMA, or the Center for Reiki Research.
7. Lunch.
8. Explain chanting and toning and the differences between them. Explain chanting goes through and around the body, and toning is for specific issues or body locations. With chanting, the energy flows wherever it goes. With toning, practitioners direct the energy with their eyes, hands and intention to go to a specific location on the client's body, aura, or energy field (*Karuna Manual*, p. 95).
9. Practice Holy Fire® and the Karuna II symbols the same as step #11 from the previous day. Decide on the time used for each symbol based on the remaining class time. You could also combine this step with chanting. Begin by chanting the symbol, then continue to practice each symbol without chanting for the remaining time. Or just do chanting for one symbol.
10. Break.
11. Explain *Healing Spirit Attachments*, go over the steps of part one and part two, and conduct a Holy Fire® Spirit Release with the class (*Karuna Manual*, pp. 53-55).
12. Cover anything remaining to be covered and ask for final questions.
13. After class, students complete their class review and email it to you.
14. Closing prayer.
15. Air hugs.

Holy Fire® III
Online Reiki Master Upgrade Class

Students who are Holy Fire® III Reiki Masters and have taken the ICRT Online Reiki training webinar entitled, *Holy Fire® Online Reiki Master Training*, or the webinar recording Upgrade class can teach this Upgrade online. Only those who already are Holy Fire® III Reiki Masters can take it. It requires approximately 6 hours to teach and will upgrade qualified students to the Holy Fire® III Online Master level for either Usui/Holy Fire® III Reiki Master or Holy Fire® III Karuna Reiki® Master. Those who take this class can teach Reiki classes both online and in person.

Topics
1. Review the history of Holy Fire® Reiki.
2. Review the philosophy and the central ideas of Holy Fire® Reiki.
3. Briefly review the history of Usui Reiki, focusing on how Usui Sensei's instruction specified that the most important activity for a Reiki practitioner is to continually seek to develop one's ability to channel ever-higher frequencies of Reiki energy.
4. Explain and conduct the *Empowered by the River of Life Experience* (p. O-23).
5. Explain Online Placements are attunements given at a distance for Reiki I and II and Usui Master Practitioner levels. Also, explain how to conduct them.
6. Explain the Online Upgrade Ignition and how it will upgrade one's Holy Fire® energy to Holy Fire® III Online and in person (p. O-25).
7. Conduct the Holy Fire® Online Ignition (p. O-25).
8. *Symbol Practice Technique* (p. O-20). Divide students into breakout rooms of 2, 3 or 4 students. Using the Distant symbol, they practice giving Holy Fire® energies to each other in sessions, using 5-10 minutes per person. One, two, or three students are giving Reiki to one. They share about this experience with each other and discuss how they experienced the energy of Holy Fire®.
9. Go over the class outlines for Holy Fire® III Online Reiki classes.
10. Review how to present the Online Experiences and the Ignitions (p. O-23).
11. Review *Online Teacher Standards of Practice, Online Student Attendance and Etiquette Standards,* and *Teacher and Student Online Etiquette* (p. O-27).
12. Review *Teacher and Student Online Preparations* and *Online Teaching Tips* (p. O-29 through p. O-37).
13. Review the *Online Technology Recommendations* (p. O-38).
14. Have a Q & A session answering questions students may have about teaching Holy Fire® III online classes, giving Reiki sessions, or questions about Reiki.
15. Close with prayers or affirmations, giving thanks for the gift of Holy Fire® Reiki and asking the Source of Reiki to guide and bless the students and their clients.

Giving an Online Holy Fire® Reiki Talk

An Online Holy Fire® Reiki Talk, as outlined here, is more than just a talk as it includes a *Holy Fire® Healing Experience*. Hosted by a Holy Fire® Reiki Master, it is an easy and enjoyable way to introduce people to Holy Fire® Reiki and experience its healing energy. You can also use this outline at a Reiki Share group or a Reiki session.

Promotion
You can make announcements on Facebook, on your website, send by email directing people back to your website announcement, and also by word of mouth. You can print hard copy flyers and post them on bulletin boards.

Location of Online Platforms
Zoom, Facebook, Facetime, Skype, and so forth.

Fee
It could be free, or a small fee could be charged to cover expenses.

Outline
1. You can have a similar set up as for an Online Reiki Circle or Share group.
2. Arrive at the online meeting room early and say prayers and become receptive to the Holy Fire® energy, asking it to clear the online space of any energies not compatible with Holy Fire® and to bless the online space.
3. Have your internet registration forms set up for people to fill out. Minimum information would be the person's name and email address.
4. When people arrive online, allow them to mill and talk. Then mute all.
5. If it's a smaller group, do introductions: name, where are you from, if they have Reiki or not. Then share air hugs.
6. A brief talk on what is Reiki.
7. Explain the evolution of Reiki and how it developed from Usui Reiki into Holy Fire® Reiki into Online Reiki.
8. Describe the qualities of Holy Fire® Reiki.
9. If there are people present who have Holy Fire® Reiki, ask if any of them would like to describe their experience of Holy Fire® Reiki or online experiences.
10. Questions and Answers.
11. Break.
12. Talk about the *Holy Fire® Healing Experience* and how it works, and explain you'll be conducting a brief guided meditation, and then stop talking for about 20 minutes. During this time, the Holy Fire® energy will be working directly with each person, providing a unique healing experience that contains what is needed by each person. Also, explain some will have inner experiences, such as seeing colors or feeling waves of healing energy flowing through them or visions of spiritual beings and so forth, and that others will simply feel relaxed, but everyone will receive something meaningful which will continue to produce benefits even after the event.
13. Conduct the *Holy Love Experience* or the *Ocean of Holy Love Experience* or the *Heavenly Banquet Hall Experience* or the *Holy Fire® Healing Experience*. Have them play Julie True's *Music to Journal By, Volume 1*, or music of their choice.
14. After bringing people back, ask them to write down their experiences, then share them if they choose to do so.
15. Close with a prayer or positive affirmation.

Online Reiki Techniques

Symbol Practice Technique—Online Practice
The Symbol Practice Technique uses distant Reiki to practice the Reiki symbols in Reiki II, Usui/Holy Fire® III Master, and Holy Fire® III Karuna Reiki® Master classes.
1. In the main room, explain that the class will divide up into small groups in breakout rooms and once in their rooms, they will make a list of each person in their group and decide who will receive first, second, third, and so forth.
2. Based on the number of students in your class, send them into breakout rooms with 2, 3 or 4 students per room.
3. Once in the breakout rooms, have them write their lists then return to the main room. If they have not returned after 10 minutes, bring them all back to the main room.
4. Have the first person to receive relax and make themselves comfortable, and the rest send them distant Reiki.
5. The teacher guides the students who are giving Reiki through each symbol for the class level they are teaching, 5-10 minutes per symbol. When doing this, have them send Reiki to the student in general, rather than sending it to a specific area of the student's body.
6. After each person, give the students time to take notes about their experience.
7. Then switch to the next person and repeat #5.
8. When all students have given and received Reiki, send the students back into the same breakout room to share about their experiences with each other and discuss how they experienced the energy of each symbol.
9. Bring everyone back to the main room and ask if they would like to share with the entire group.

Giving a Complete Distant Reiki Session—Online Technique Practice
1. For Reiki II: explain Distant Reiki is done during the Symbol Practice Technique.
2. For Reiki Master classes: in Reiki Master and Karuna Master, review Online Distant Reiki. Refer to the techniques in *Reiki, The Healing Touch*, page 50.
3. Review and use the *Giving a Complete Reiki Session* guidelines (*Healing Touch*, p. 91).
4. Divide students into breakout rooms of two people each.
5. One student is the client, the other is the practitioner.
6. Make sure the client is comfortable while receiving.
7. The practitioner asks the client if they have a particular area of concern, and intention.
8. The practitioner activates the Distant symbol and each of the Reiki symbols and sends Reiki to both the practitioner's and client's space.
9. The practitioner gives a complete distance session.
10. The practitioner can send distance Gyoshi-ho and Byosen scanning using a Teddy bear or dummy to represent the person.
11. Practitioners can give the complete Reiki session using a surrogate such as a Teddy bear, pillow, dummy, or another surrogate of their choice.

12. When the session is complete, seal with CKR or HF.
13. The practitioner uses the Kenyoku technique at the end.
14. The teacher notifies the students, using text, when to complete their session and share their experience and switch.
15. The client becomes the practitioner, and the practitioner becomes the client.
16 When done, bring all students back to the main room and share.

Distant Gyoshi-ho Technique

Review Gyoshi-ho (*Healing Touch*, p. 62). Explain that a practitioner can use this in a distant or an in-person session.

1. Have students divide into groups of two and enter a breakout room.
2. One student is the client, the other is the practitioner.
3. For Reiki II: the practitioner activates HSZSN.
4. For Reiki Master classes: the practitioner activates the Holy Fire® Master symbol.
5. Use Byosen scanning or Reiji-ho or the request of the client to decide where you are going to send Reiki.
6. You can also use this process without using Byosen by sending Reiki to the whole person.
7. Draw the Power symbol on your hands and place them on your legs and let Reiki start flowing.
8. Then focus your eyes onto the area in need and intend Reiki to flow from your eyes to the client.
9. Allow your eyes to relax.
10. You can also use your hands to beam Reiki to the area.
11. As you do this, meditate on Reiki energy and on your eyes, and intend that Reiki flow from your eyes to the area.
12. If any thoughts arise, gently brush them aside and refocus your intention.
13. Do this for several minutes or longer.

To practice this technique in class:
1. Divide students into breakout rooms of two people each.
2. One student is the client, one is the practitioner.
3. Make sure the client is comfortable and receptive.
4. Have students practice distant Gyoshi-ho for 10 minutes each.
5. Text students when time is up. Give them time to share their experiences, then switch.
6. Text them when it is time to come back to the main room.

Explain that Gyoshi-ho can be used by itself, or during a complete session online or in person. When intending that you are using hand positions, such as on a dummy, give Reiki to one body area with your hands and another area with your eyes. The practitioner may experience shifts in their perceptions of their client, such as changes in gender, age, lifetimes, and so forth. But as best you can, do not allow this to startle you, and simply continue with the session, remaining with your eyes de-focused.

Enkaku Chiryo Online Technique
1. Explain how the Chat works on Zoom. While you're in a Zoom meeting, you can chat with other participants. You can send a group chat message or send a private message to an individual.
2. Explain Enkaku Chiryo (*Healing Touch*, p. 62).
3. Ask the students to place the names of those they would like to send distant Reiki to into the Chat on the Zoom panel.
4. The entire class sends distance Reiki to the people and events written in the Chat.
5. It can also include projects, goals, world issues, other countries, or for the entire planet. Have the class send Reiki to the issues in the Chat for 5-10 minutes or more. Share experiences.

Energy Clearing Technique—Online Practice
Have students divide into groups of two and choose who will receive first. The practitioner activates their Reiki hands. Using the image of your partner on the screen, place your hands above and to the side of your partner's head. Motion your hands up and down an inch or two and slowly move downward from the head to the feet, intending you are clearing the client's energy field. If you feel a block, stay at the blocked area until you feel it releasing or that your hands are moving through the block, and then when you get to the floor, slap the floor three times with your hands. Now imagine you are standing to the side of the client. Repeat the energy clearing motion from the side. Finish with air hugs.
1. Divide students into breakout rooms of two people each.
2. One student does the energy clearing technique at a time, then switches.
3. When both are finished, they complete with air hugs.
4. Text the students to return to the main room when finished.

Holy Fire® Affirmation
This simple affirmation will help to unify your consciousness and more strongly connect you with your Authentic Self. Repeat this throughout your day to establish the clarity and strength of your Authentic Self more firmly as your personal identity.
1. Activate Holy Fire® in your hands.
2. Draw the Holy Fire® symbol (or the Power symbol if you have not received the Holy Fire® symbol yet) in front of you or simply become aware of it.
3. Say to yourself with total confidence and assertion, "I am my Authentic Self."

Air Hugs
1. People love air hugs!
2. Reach through the computer, hug each person to greet them and at the end of class.

Online Experiences and Ignitions

Empowered by the River of Life Experience
This Experience is used to give Holy Fire® Master students the ability to give Online Placements when they teach, to` use the *Holy Fire® Online Healing Experience*, and to facilitate the Online *Empowered by the River of Life Experience* in their own Master classes. It is used in the Usui/Holy Fire® Online Master class and the Holy Fire® Online Karuna Reiki® Master class. This Experience will also allow all those students who teach other styles of Reiki in person to continue to do so. This ability is possible because this Experience will empower the student with the Holy Fire® in such a way so that it works in harmony with the other systems of Reiki a student may have.

Students can be seated or lying on the floor and can change positions during the experience if they choose to. Ask the students to relax. Have them start their music, such as Julie True's *Music to Journal By, Volume 1*, or any music that is soothing and meditative for them.

Use This Script to Explain the River of Life
"There is a sacred mountain range where the peaks of the mountains reach up energetically into the higher heavens. The rain and snow that fall on these mountains come from the highest spiritual heaven. This water flows down the mountains and over beautiful waterfalls then flows together to form a sacred river. The river also flows through a volcanic area where it is warmed to jacuzzi temperature. The water in the River of Life is crystal clear and completely pure and unites us with the Earth's sacred energy. It also unites us with all living things. It awakens us to our authentic human spirit; our authentic human gifts, talents, skills, and higher consciousness are revealed in our daily life. A new sense of belonging fills our sense of wellbeing. Because the river comes from the highest heavens, you will be able to breathe underwater. And when you breathe the water, the sacred water flows completely through you, healing and refreshing every part of your being. There are also flames underwater and on the surface. These are the living flames of the Holy Fire®, which do not burn but are soothing, purifying, healing, guiding, and empowering. You may have other beautiful experiences not mentioned here."

Master Class Information
If you teach this as part of either of the Master classes, add this information in your talk. "The River of Life Experience also gives you the ability to conduct Online Experiences and Placements or do them in person. This process is so powerful that even if you simply read the Experiences from the book, they will work just fine. But it would be better if you practiced them until you have them memorized as it will allow you to enter the flow of the Experience better yourself."

Follow this script to present the teacher-guided portion of the Experience. Please understand that the word "Pause" in the script is not to be read to the class but is guidance for *you* to pause a moment to give the students time to experience what you are guiding them to do.

1. "Imagine it is a beautiful sunny day. Imagine you are barefoot walking through a beautiful forest." (Pause.)
2. "As you breathe into yourself, imagine you are breathing in the life essence of the forest. And with each step you take, imagine the Earth's energies are flowing up through the bottoms of your feet." (Pause.)
3. "As you walk along, allow yourself to experience the trees, plants, flowers and grass, and to merge with the life and the harmony and peace of the forest." (Pause.)
4. "As you continue to walk along, you notice that up ahead, it is getting lighter, and you realize you are coming to the edge of the forest."
5. "As you leave the forest, before you is a beautiful river. It is the River of Life. Beautiful flowers are growing along the riverbank, and there is a path following alongside the river. Follow the path alongside the river."
6. "As you walk along the path, you feel the beautiful energy of the sacred water and feel yourself becoming one with all living things." (Pause.)
7. "Eventually, you come to a place where you can easily enter the water. You pause at the water's edge and realize this river contains the life energy that flows through all living things. You drink from the River of Life and feel the essence of life flow through you. You realize you are one with all living things. And this gives you a sense of belonging."
8. "You enter the water completely. Feel it flowing around you."
9. "The light from the highest heavens is shining on you as you swim and float and dive into the river's depth."
10. "The River of Life is guiding you now. Allow yourself to be guided by the River of Life."

Stop talking. At this time, you can say silent prayers to Jesus, God, and the Holy Spirit, indicating that you completely surrender the experiences of the students and yourself over to Jesus, God, the Holy Spirit, to the Brothers and Sisters of the Light, and the Ascended Masters. You can say additional prayers asking that the students receive the greatest healing and blessings God can create, or other similar prayers. Then after saying prayers, simply direct your attention inwardly and allow yourself to be guided by the River of Life.

Using a timer or stopwatch, wait 15-25 minutes or so. Then gently bring the students back with words such as these:

1. "You can continue with your experience as long as you feel guided to do so."
2. "Whenever you are ready, take a couple of deep breaths and bring your attention to your eyes."
3. "Then, slowly open your eyes and come back."
4. After a minute, say, "Take some time to write about your experiences in your notebooks." After everyone has stopped writing, ask, "Who would like to share?"

Holy Fire® Online Ignitions

The third and fourth Online Ignitions have a specific energy that ignites and reveals your Divine Spirit. The energy was given to us to unify our divine spirit with our human spirit in our daily life. It also is specifically given to us to integrate the spiritual guidance of distance Reiki with the enlightened life force energy of technology and the internet. It provides a heightened sense of innovation, empowerment, a unification of self and with others, and unlimited possibilities.

There Are Still Four Ignitions Given

Procedure for the First and Second Master Ignitions
Unlike Holy Fire® II, there is no pre-Ignition in Holy Fire® III. Instead, an Ignition replaces the pre-Ignition for a total of four Ignitions. The new class outlines reflect this change. Students can lay on the floor or a couch or sit in a chair as each chooses. It is also permissible for students to change their position during the Ignition process if they feel the need to do so. Meditation music can play in the background. Let the students know that they can follow your direction at the beginning, but at any time even as you continue to give guidance, they may begin being guided inwardly by the Holy Fire®. If this happens, it's okay for them to follow their inner guidance.

Script
1. Spoken slowly with appropriate pauses: "Take a deep breath and close your eyes. Bring your hands up into the Gassho position. Now focus your attention on the space between your palms. If thoughts arise in your mind, gently brush them aside and bring your attention back to the space between your palms."

2. Wait for 1-2 minutes and continue with: "A beautiful light appears high up in the heavens. The light comes down, descending all the way down to in front of your hands, then flows through your hands and into your heart. The gift of Love."

3. "The Ignition process has begin now. Remain with your eyes closed and your attention focused inwardly on your own inner experience. (Pause) Open your heart and receive as the light of your Authentic Self is revealed."

Then stop speaking and wait 20-26 minutes. During this time say prayers giving thanks for the experiences the Holy Fire® is providing to each student, and spend time going inward and being in your own experience.

Keep track of the time using a clock or cell phone set to airplane mode, or use another kind of timer. When you sense it is time for the students to come back say words to this effect: "Whenever you feel ready to return, take a few breaths, bring your awareness to your eyes and slowly open your eyes and come back."

After most are back, ask them to take time to write down their experiences and to integrate.

Wait until all students finish writing, then ask, "Who would like to share his or her experience?"

Procedure for the Third and Fourth Online Master Ignitions

Students can lay on the floor or a couch, or sit in a chair, as each chooses. It is also permissible for students to change their position during the Ignition process if they feel the need to do so. Meditation music can play in the background. Let the students know that they can follow your direction at the beginning, but at any time, even as you continue to give guidance, they may begin being guided inwardly by the Holy Fire®. If this happens, it's okay for them to follow their inner guidance.

Follow the same Ignition process as described on page 93 in the *Usui/Holy Fire® III Reiki Master Manual*, except in the second two Ignitions, substitute the numbered directions in the Master manual with these below.

1. Spoken slowly with appropriate pauses: "Take a deep breath and close your eyes. Place your palms up resting on your legs or somewhere comfortable." (Pause.)
2. "Focus on being receptive." (Pause.) "The Ignition process will begin now. Remain with your eyes closed and your attention focused inwardly on your own inner experience. **Go within, open your heart, and receive.** [Say to the students] **Say the following words to yourself, 'I am my Authentic Self.'**"

Then stop talking and wait 20-26 minutes. During this time, you can say prayers giving thanks for the experiences the Holy Fire® is providing to each student, and spend time going inward and being in your own experience.

Keep track of time. When you sense it is time for your students to come back, say, "Take as long as you like, and when you are ready to come back, bring your awareness to your eyes, then slowly open your eyes and come back. **As you come back, say to yourself, 'I am my Authentic Self.'** Take this time to write about your experience and integrate." Wait until all finish writing, then ask, "Who would like to share their experience?"

Online Teaching Best Practices

Online Teacher Standards

While we are using the internet to connect with our students and to teach, all the material must be taught live by the teacher using their online device. We recommend that you teach about the same number of students you typically teach in your in-person classes. This decision is so that you are able to provide individual attention for each student, and answer questions and allow students to share with each other.

1. Use the same professionalism online as in person.
2. Be sure you can see all students at the same time on one screen on your computer.
3. Use the digital versions of *Holy Fire® III Reiki Master Online and In-Person* manuals, containing the *Reiki Master Training Online* section. Make sure each student receives their manual before the class.
4. Use the Online Class Outlines provided in the *Reiki Master Training Online* section.
5. Classes need to contain about the same number of hours as recommended in the RMA *Standards of Practice* on page 145 of the Reiki Master Manual, and page 100 of the Karuna Reiki® Manual.
6. Follow all the other guidelines in the *Code of Ethics and Standards of Practice* in the Holy Fire® III Master Manuals.

Online Student Attendance and Etiquette Standards

Online students must attend the class in person online, with their video on during all class time, and not be engaged in any other online activities. They must participate in all parts of the class. We have provided a sample email you can send to your Reiki students to prepare them for class attendance, located on page O-33.

Teacher and Student Online Etiquette

1. Behave as if you are in an in-person class.
2. Be present during the entire class.
3. Use video during the entire class.
4. Participate in all class activities.
5. Use a quiet private place for your participation in the class.
6. Use a separate room, so not bothered by your family or pets.
7. Make sure other members of your household know you will be busy and not available during class time. Ask them to be quiet as you will be in class.
8. Refrain from doing other things while in class.
9. Refrain from being on other online apps or devices during class.
10. Make sure you are comfortable and that you are in front of your screen within view of your camera while in class.
11. Use mute during the Experiences, Placements and Ignitions so background noise will not bother the other students.
12. Chat etiquette: Please be considerate on Chat. Stay on topic, ask questions, or make relevant comments.

13. Come back promptly from the breaks and lunch. The class will not begin until all are present. You will hold up class for the other students if you do not return from breaks and lunch on time.

Teacher and Student Online Preparations

Preparations to Teach Online Reiki Classes

You will need to prepare to teach online. To begin, you will need a computer, the internet, video, microphone, and an online video conferencing app. Below we have technology and equipment recommendations. We recommend the Zoom online video conference application (www.zoom.us).

It is essential to become familiar with the Zoom features you will need for your online class. We have provided helpful Zoom tutorial links below to features such as Mute, Unmute, the Chat, Breakout Rooms, and Screen Share. However, you will need to explore Zoom for yourself before class. Watch the Zoom tutorials and YouTube videos to learn the application and also to gain helpful hints from others with more experience. Practice with friends and family. We recommend you also practice using Zoom with your students before your class to make sure they have the online access they need to attend. Ask students to arrive online early before class to check-in to make sure all are ready, so your class begins on time.

Practice the Online Outlines and Online Techniques used in each class level before teaching it. Consider how you are going to demonstrate the hand positions in Reiki I, practice the symbols in Reiki II and the Master and Karuna Master levels, and show the Peace Grid in the Master class.

Online Video Classroom

You need to establish your online classroom and setting. Your webcam will video you and the background behind you. Dress comfortably, but professionally. Choose a comfortable chair. Good lighting, sound, and video make a difference in your presentation. However, start with what you own and improve your equipment as you go. There are recommendations in the *Online Technology Recommendations* section.

Preparation and practice will give you confidence in teaching your online classes. It is normal to have technical "glitches" during the day. It is okay; everyone understands. You will soon learn the common issues that occur and the solutions for them, just like teaching in person. You will continue to think of new ideas about how to conduct your Online Reiki class, so try them out. Continue doing the things that work and stop doing the things that don't work.

PowerPoints and Videos

Zoom has a screen sharing feature, so you can use a PowerPoint, make pre-made videos, and use photos to demonstrate a technique. If you use a PowerPoint, we recommend showing the slide, but then stop the screen share and continue talking about the subject. Students report they like it best when you toggle back and forth between you and the PowerPoint.

Recommendations Prior to Online Class
1. Set up a computer, video, audio.
2. Install the Zoom application on your computer.
3. The free account only allows a 40-minute meeting with three or more people, so you will need the Pro Account for $14.99 per month, for up to 100 people, with unlimited meeting time. https://zoom.us/pricing.
4. Watch the Zoom tutorials for the most used tools, and watch Zoom videos produced by others on YouTube. The following links are for your convenience. Zoom also provides live training.
    a. **A Complete Beginners Guide 2020** is beneficial to watch, even if you are experienced: www.youtube.com/watch?v=xcEXn4mnyLM.
    b. **Zoom Help Center:** https://support.zoom.us/hc/en-us.
    c. **Getting Started:** https://support.zoom.us/hc/en-us/categories/200101697.
    d. **How to Schedule a Meeting:** https://support.zoom.us/hc/en-us/articles/201362413-Scheduling-meetings.
    e. **Meeting Controls:** Mute, unmute, video on/off: https://www.youtube.com/watch?v=ygZ96J_z4AY&feature=emb_rel_pause.
    f. **Managing the Participant Panel:** https://support.zoom.us/hc/en-us/articles/115005759423-Managing-participants-in-a-meeting.
    g. **Testing Computer or Devise Audio:** https://support.zoom.us/hc/en-us/articles/201362283-Testing-computer-or-device-audio.
    h. **Using an In-Meeting Chat on the Sidebar:** https://support.zoom.us/hc/en-us/articles/203650445-In-Meeting-Chat.
    i. **Enabling Video Breakout Rooms:** https://support.zoom.us/hc/en-us/articles/206476093-Getting-Started-with-Video-Breakout-Rooms.
    j. **Sharing Your Screen:** https://support.zoom.us/hc/en-us/articles/206476093-Getting-Started-with-Video-Breakout-Rooms.
    k. **Virtual Backgrounds:** https://www.youtube.com/watch?reload=9&v=3Zq-b51A3dA. Virtual backgrounds can use extra bandwidth. If you have trouble with your video or internet connection during class, turn this feature off and see if it is the issue.
    l. **Zoom Training Resources:** https://zoom.us/docs/en-us/covid19.html.
    m. **Another Good Beginner Tutorial:** https://www.youtube.com/watch?v=hI32Xk2Va7M.
    n. **Zoom Security Recommendations:** https://zoom.us/security.
    o. **Zoom Meeting Security Tutorial for Reiki Practitioners and Teachers:** https://www.youtube.com/watch?v=uQGffwK62T4&t=388s.
5. Schedule your Zoom meetings when you schedule your Reiki class. Send the information in the email to your students at least the week before class.
6. Send another reminder email on the morning of the class.
7. Test your audio and video.
8. Create your video background, backdrop.
9. Establish a quiet, private location from which to teach.
10. Have someone else take care of your children and pets.

11. Email digital copy manuals, or mail hard copy manuals to your students as soon as they sign up. See the section on how to use USPS to mail from home.
12. Email student preparations before class. See the following *Sample Email to Students*.
13. Read the Reiki class manual and use the Holy Fire® Online section.
14. Practice *Online Techniques* and demonstrations.
15. Establish how you will receive payments.

Teaching Recommendations at the Beginning of Class
1. Test the audio and video before each class begins.
2. Keep your computer plugged in.
3. Minimize background noise.
4. Hold your class in a quiet, private place.
5. Set up your space and background.
6. Be comfortable.
7. Put the Reiki symbols all around your room.
8. Print your roster.
9. tart early to make sure everyone is able to get online.
10. Explain how to use the Zoom features used in class: Mute, Unmute, Chat, video on and off, hand raising.
11. Here is an example of the explanation you may give at the beginning of a class.
    a. In larger classes explain they will be on mute because of background noise. Smaller classes may be able to stay unmuted.
    b. You will have people who are not familiar with technology, so be simple with your directions.
    c. Always put everyone on mute and explain how this works, that there will be background noises: "Hover over your own picture to unmute, or mute, or stop your video on the bottom of the screen." They are welcome to mute and unmute anytime to ask questions or share.
    d. If you have a question and want to ask, you can raise your hands on the bottom in the participant panel. The host can lower a hand or lower all hands.
    e. Calling in by phone, *6 is the command for mute and unmute.
    f. Swiping left or right on phones will give other control options.
    g. There is also a Chat feature; a student can enter a question or comment into the Chat.
    h. They can send a private chat or public message.
    i. If you are the host, you have an option to unmute and mute all or individually in the button in the participant panel. This ability will give you more control.
    j. You can share links to files in the Chat.
    k. Have meetings in the gallery view, or speaker view, controlled at the top right of the Zoom window.
12. Greeting your students.
    a. Unmute all and let everyone say hello and good morning at the same time.
    b. When doing introductions, unmute one person at a time.

c. On the second and third days, you may unmute each person, have them say their name and where they are from. Have everyone greet them and say good morning even if they are all on mute. If it is a small group, you may be able to have unmute on.
d. Invite people to share as you normally would.

Student Preparations

Inform your Reiki students what they will need to prepare for your online Reiki class. They will need a computer, tablet, or smartphone with audio and video capabilities. They will need to install Zoom and review Zoom instructions.

Mail class manuals to students and emphasize the need to read it. Email symbols to your students for Reiki II and the Master classes and inform them they need to be prepared to take a test on the symbols.

Recommend students use a Teddy bear or dummy for hand positions and distant practice. For the Master class, students need a crystal or stone for the Peace Grid. Provide music recommendations and *Online Attendance and Etiquette* information, so they know what to expect. See the following sample email to use as a template.

Sample Emails to Students

We have provided the following sample email with important information your students need to prepare for their Reiki class, and a sample of a follow-up email you can send after the class. Use these as a template to write your own. The parentheses are places where you need to include your information.

Usui/Holy Fire® III Online Reiki I & II Workshop
Reminder and Confirmation

Hi Everyone,

I am looking forward to meeting all of you in the Reiki I and II workshop on (date). **Please** RSVP and confirm that you are attending by emailing me at (email address). Also, please confirm the spelling of your name and how you want it on your Reiki certificate.

(Names of students here):

Reminders
- Download the zoom.us application: https://zoom.us/support/download.
- The Zoom Help Center presents information on getting started: https://support.zoom.us/hc/en-us/categories/200101697-Getting-Started.
- Watch the Zoom tutorial on joining a meeting: https://support.zoom.us/hc/en-us/articles/201362193-How-Do-I-Join-A-Meeting.
- Here is another good tutorial on how to use Zoom, for beginners: https://www.youtube.com/watch?v=9isp3qPeQ0E.
- Practice using Zoom prior to class.
- You will need a computer, tablet, or smartphone with audio and video.
- The class is all day. If you are on a tablet or smartphone, it is recommended that you put them on a tripod.
- Balance Due: If you have a balance due, you will be sent an invoice via (list method) _____. Please pay the balance before class to save class time.
- Manual: Your Manual, *Reiki, The Healing Touch*, was mailed to you. Go ahead and begin reading it now, if possible. **The Reiki II symbols are attached**. Please practice drawing the symbols and writing the names of the symbols. I will ask you to draw and spell them by memory on the second day of class.
- Class time: 9 A.M.–6:30 P.M. each day. Please come at 8:30 to get settled with technology and your personal comfort. Clarify your time zone.
- Lunch & Breaks: We will have a 1-hour lunch, and multiple breaks will be provided.
- Preparation: Dress comfortably, be in a private area where you won't be disturbed during class, use the restroom before class and during breaks.

Recommended Items to Have on Hand
1. Reiki Manual

2. Notebook/journal, pen
3. Earbuds
4. Water/snack
5. Music (Include sample links to Julie True, Calamaria, YouTube, Spotify, personal calm music.)
6. Blanket/pillow/comfort items

Reiki I
1. Have something or someone on which to practice your hand positions, such as a Teddy bear, family member, or a surrogate of your choice.

Reiki Master Classes: The Reiki Grid
1. Download a Peace Grid from reiki.org; Free Peace Grid Download, Letter-Size Peace Grid, https://www.reiki.org/resources/reiki-grid-instructions-using-world-peace-crystal-grid.
2. Laminated Peace Grid: https://www.reiki.org/store/prints-and-posters/reiki-grid-using-world-peace-crystal-grid.
3. Have a crystal or stone to imbue.

Online Student Attendance Requirements and Etiquette Guidelines
1. Plan to have someone else take care of the kids and pets.
2. Plan to attend the entire class.
3. Participate in all activities.
4. Use video during all classes.
5. Behave as if you are in an in-person class.
6. If you wouldn't do something in person, don't do it online.
7. Refrain from doing other things online during class, such as checking email, texting, getting up and wandering around. Refrain from moving around while on video. It is distracting for others.
8. Here is the Zoom meeting information: (Insert your information.)
9. Click on the link below to join a class (include link information, see the following example).

Note: This is just a sample for your email; it will not link your students to your meeting.
Join Zoom Meeting
Colleen Benelli is inviting you to a scheduled Zoom meeting.

Join Zoom Meeting
https://reikilifestyle.zoom.us/j/9474256689

Meeting ID: 947 425 6689

One tap mobile
+13462487799,,9474256689# US (Houston)
+14086380968,,9474256689# US (San Jose)

Dial by your location
    +1 346 248 7799 US (Houston)
    +1 408 638 0968 US (San Jose)
    +1 669 900 6833 US (San Jose)
    +1 646 876 9923 US (New York)
    +1 253 215 8782 US
    +1 301 715 8592 US
    +1 312 626 6799 US (Chicago)
Meeting ID: 947 425 6689
Find your local number: https://reikilifestyle.zoom.us/u/adXa2WPItN

If calling the morning of the class, please call (phone number). My email address is (email).

See you soon!

Many Blessings,
Name of teacher
Website address

Sample Email to Send as a Follow-Up
Usui/Holy Fire® III Reiki I and II Workshop Follow-Up

Hi Everyone,

Please stay in touch! You may want to contact your other classmates to practice and share Reiki! I have attached documents for our class and listed website and resource listings below:
1. Class Certificate
2. Class Photo (online screenshot of all students on the screen at once.)
3. Student Class List (Roster)
4. Lineage Chart (Attach the Word document for a student to add their name.)

Website and Resources: (Add links for your resources below.)
1. Website (your website)
2. Reiki Master Workshop (Date they are eligible to take in 6 months)
3. Monthly Reiki Circle (place link)
4. Personal Reiki sessions
5. Facebook page
6. Instagram page
7. YouTube video channel

International Center for Reiki Training (We talk about the ICRT in our classes; it is nice to have links so they can find them easily. This is optional.)
1. William Rand's website is a great resource for more Reiki information and articles: www.reiki.org.
2. International Center for Reiki Training Facebook page: www.facebook.com/internationalcenterforreikitraining
3. ICRT Instagram page: www.instagram.com/icrtofficial/
4. The World Peace Grid Meditation Project/World Peace Card Meditation Project www.reiki.org/world-peace-grid-project, & www.reiki.org/world-peace-card-meditation
5. *Reiki News Magazine*: www.reiki.org/store/reiki-news-magazine
6. Center for Reiki Research and Reiki in Hospitals Information: www.centerforreikiresearch.org

Many Blessings,
Name of teacher
Website address

Online Teaching Tips

Be prepared with the online demonstrations and techniques you will teach. Have your music very low or off during Experiences and Ignitions. You may have it on during the silence, just mute your computer.

Hand Positions for Reiki II: Options for Practice
1. Order a dummy, set up a table.
2. Show hand positions in *Reiki, The Healing Touch*, page 83.
3. Have a family member be on the table.
4. Use a Teddy bear.

Peace Grid, Crystal Practice for Reiki Master
1. Hold a photo up to the camera.
2. Take a photo of yours and screen share.
3. Get a Peace Grid for Reiki Master and set it up with a hard backing so you can move it. If you use crystals, glue them to the grid.

Symbol Test
1. Call on students one at a time.
2. Student holds their symbols with symbol names up to the camera.
3. Gently ask them to make corrections if needed.

Class Reviews
1. Email reviews prior to class.
2. Students email their reviews back to the teacher at the end of class.

Certificates
1. Screen share a certificate from class.
2. Celebrate the students receiving their certificates.
3. Mail the certificate to the student after receiving the review.

Practice the *Online Techniques* in the Holy Fire® Online Reiki Master Training Section
1. Symbol Practice Technique
2. Distance Reiki Technique
3. Enkaku Chiryo Practice
4. Gyoshi-ho Practice
5. Practice presenting the *Empowered by the River of Life Experience*

Online Technology Recommendations

The following are some recommendations that have been successful for us. You may use your own way of video-conferencing and teaching in-person and online Reiki classes. Please refer to the online resources and tutorials from Zoom for additional technical assistance.

Internet Connection
We recommend that you hardwire your internet connection (use an ethernet cable to directly plug your computer into your internet connection). This step will help you avoid any issues with an unstable Wi-Fi connection which can affect your audio quality and the overall experience of your students. It will also increase the speed. If you have connection difficulties, it may lie in using too much bandwidth. Check with your internet provider for more information about your internet speed.

Zoom Meeting versus Webinar
Use a Zoom meeting for your Reiki classes. A Zoom meeting gives you the ability to engage with each of your students personally, see them on the screen, and they can each talk with the others. The Zoom breakout rooms give you the ability to separate your students into private rooms of two or more people. The screen share feature gives you the ability to show your students what is on your screen.

A webinar is different because you have limited interaction with your students. A webinar is like a presentation on stage where you are talking *to* your students rather than *with* them.

Online Equipment Recommendations
Your equipment makes a difference. This list is what has been successful for us. There may be other options. Some choices may be out of stock. Use what you have and get these items when you can. It is okay to improve as you go.

Computer, Internet Devices
1. You will need a computer to teach online Reiki.
2. Some people use a tablet successfully.
3. It would be more challenging to teach from a smartphone.

Microphone and Audio
Good sound quality makes a difference. This aspect is a higher priority.
1. Get a "condenser microphone." Amazon has many options and prices.
2. We like the Blue Yeti Microphone. On Amazon for about $129.

Your Sound
1. You may have your own preference in listening online. You can use your computer speakers or your earbuds or headphones, etc.
2. Make sure you are comfortable and can hear your students well.

Webcam and Video
1. Good images make a difference.
2. An HD webcam typically provides a better image than your computer camera. We use the Logitech HD 1080 or similar. If these are out of stock, or the price is very high, continue to check for availability on Amazon, Best Buy, etc. It is also fine to use your computer camera if that is all you have. You can get an HD webcam later.

Tripod
1. A tripod is just for ease. It is not necessary and a webcam mounted on the back of a laptop screen works great.
2. You can easily move and direct a camera on a lightweight tripod. It is easier to move a tripod than your computer. There are good inexpensive, lightweight tripods available on Amazon.
3. It is possible just to use your computer camera. The webcam and tripod add simplicity.

Optional Tips
The following items are optional but make things easier.
1. An HDMI cable hooks your computer to a TV. You can see everyone on your TV screen. But when you use the keyboard, you look away from the camera.
2. Two USB 12-foot extension cords. USB extension cords for your camera and microphone make it makes it easier to move your microphone and your camera around.
3. Get a USB adapter if you need more USB ports to accommodate your equipment.

Ship from Home

We recommend that you sign up on www.usps.com and ship your Reiki Manuals to your students from home. It may be slightly more expensive, but beneficial at this time of social distancing. They will deliver the shipping supplies you need. You can purchase a postage scale on Amazon, weigh your package, and pay the shipping cost online. Note: If shipping from home is an issue for you, or if you are outside of the US, please email center@reiki.org. They will investigate additional shipping options for you.

Shipping from Home with USPS—Helpful Tips
1. Go to https://reg.usps.com/ to set up an account.
2. Once you are logged in, click Mail & Ship in the top blue bar and choose Click-N-Ship from the drop-down.
3. *Where are you sending from?* Setup the return address to be your business name and address so you will always have this information available.
4. *Where are you sending to?* Follow the steps to create the label with the name and address of the person you are sending to.
5. *Enter a Shipping Date.* Choose the date you wish to ship.
6. *Enter Package Details.* Choose, "I am shipping Flat Rate" unless you are making international shipments, then you will need package weight, size, and value.
7. *Enter Package Value.* Skip unless this is an international shipment.
8. *Select a Service type.* Choose Priority Mail and click on the blue bar for *Next: Select a Service Type.*
9. Choose the **Flat Rate envelope**. It is important to use Flat Rate for manuals because of the weight. Check the current price for mailing on usps.com.
10. *Add Insurance and extra services.* This is your choice, and you can see the options available to you.
11. Click on the blue bar for *Add to Cart.*
12. You can check out from here (click on the blue bar: *Next Billing Information*) or add another label for another package by starting back at step 2. We suggest you only do ten labels at a time before checking out.
13. You will have the ability to print the labels on plain paper with a receipt once you have checked out and paid for all labels.

Note: From the home page, you can click Mail & Ship, and the drop-down menu will give you the option to have supplies delivered for free and set up a pickup for packages you wish to ship. We use the Priority Mail Flat Rate envelope for one manual and to keep the costs down. Here is the link for the one we use to copy and paste into your browser after logging into your account: https://store.usps.com/store/product/shipping-supplies/priority-mail-flat-rate-envelope-ep14f-P_EP_14_F. Copy and paste into your browser once you are logged into your account.

Questions and Answers
Holy Fire® Online Reiki Master Upgrade Class

Q. Will I be able to teach all my Reiki classes online after taking this class?

A. Yes. We have Online class outlines for all the Holy Fire® online classes. You will be able to teach the same Holy Fire® classes online that you are currently qualified to teach in person.

Q. How can you teach Reiki classes online? Don't the Placements and Ignitions need to be given in person?

A. The Placements and Ignitions needed to be given in person in the past. But, the Brothers and Sisters of the Light saw the problems that the coronavirus was creating and formulated a higher frequency Reiki energy that allows one to teach online. William Rand and Colleen Benelli were given this new Ignition and the specific details needed to teach this class. This new energy is provided in the new Holy Fire® Online Reiki Master Upgrade class.

Q. Why can't we just begin teaching online now? Why do we need to take your class?

A. Because the energy of the previous Holy Fire® classes did not have a high enough frequency for us to effectively give the Ignitions at a distance. And also, we were not ready to receive the higher-level energy. But because we have been using Holy Fire® energy all this time, our energy has evolved to the point that we are ready. This evolution is the same as in the past when the ever-higher levels of Holy Fire® energy were given to us progressively over time in previous Holy Fire® upgrade classes.

Q. Will I still be able to teach in person?

A. Yes. There is no requirement that after taking this class that you must teach only online. You will continue to be able to teach in person too.

Q. I have extra Reiki manuals; what can I do with them if I start teaching online classes?

A. The same Holy Fire® III manuals are used in the online classes but with the addition of a supplement that includes revised class outlines and the additional instruction needed. The supplement is sent to you for downloading when you sign up for the class. So, if you have Holy Fire® II manuals, you will be able to use them.

Q. How much should I charge for online classes?

A. We suggest that you charge the same amount that you have been charging for your in-person classes because, with our current level of technology, the classes are easily and effectively taught online. And also, the online method is convenient for your students as there is no travel time. In addition, even though world travel and personal contact are limited by the coronavirus pandemic, your students will also be able to continue practicing and teaching and earning an income.

Q. Are class certificates available for the online classes?
A. Yes, they are available to Professional members on the Reiki Membership website.

Q. If classes are online, wouldn't most students want to take their Reiki classes from William Rand and the other experienced teachers making it difficult for most teachers to find students?
A. William and the other Licensed Reiki Master Teachers plan to teach about the same number of students as they have in the past, so this shouldn't be a problem.

Q. I don't know much about computers; how will I be able to do this?
A. Included in this class is a tutorial on how to use your computer to teach online classes.

Q. Why is your online training class so expensive?
A. The price is based on the value of what is being taught. For example, after taking the Upgrade class, you will be able to continue teaching your classes and earning income.

Q. Does the new Ignition provide only the ability to teach online, or does it have other benefits?
A. Yes, in addition to giving you the ability to teach online, the new Ignition will upgrade your Holy Fire® energy as well, making it stronger and more apparent in how it is blessing your life.

Q. How can I tell if I should take this class?
A. If you are asking this question, we suggest that you carefully re-read the information, and if you are still not sure, we suggest that you meditate about it and let your intuition guide you.

Registered Holy Fire® III Karuna Reiki® Master Training Manual
In-Person

Holy Fire® III Karuna Reiki®

By taking this class, all your Reiki classes will be upgraded to Holy Fire® III. This includes Reiki I, II, Reiki Master and Karuna. Attunements will no longer be given. Instead, placements will be given for Reiki I, II and the first part of Reiki Master. Placements will be given and in the Usui Reiki Master and the Karuna Master classes, Ignitions will be given. Instructions on how to give Placements and Ignitions are included in this manual and are taught in class. In addition, the class outlines for all the classes are also included. In the Karuna class, the energies of all the symbols have been upgraded to be Holy Fire® III energies making them more refined and effective.

Karuna is a Sanskrit word and is used in Hinduism, Buddhism and Zen. It is translated to indicate any action that is taken to diminish the suffering of others and or more specifically means "compassionate action." When individuals experience enlightenment, they report that all beings are known as one. Therefore, it is natural to extend compassionate action or Karuna to everyone without distinction because we are all one. As we help others and aid them in their healing process, all beings benefit. Because of the oneness of all beings, it is understood that Karuna is not only extended to others out of love, but also because it is an entirely logical thing to do. In the same way that you would want to heal your own wounds, you would also want the wounds of others to heal.

Karuna is the motivating quality of all beings in the third heaven or higher who are working to end all suffering on earth. They continually send an unlimited amount of healing energy and guidance to us, but not all are receptive to it. As you develop Karuna in yourself, not only are you helping others, but you also become more receptive to the Karuna that is being sent. Thus your healing is quickened. Karuna Reiki® opens you to work directly with the higher heavens.

Origin of the Holy Fire® Karuna System of Reiki
This system of Reiki has evolved over time. Karuna Reiki® which was the first expression of this class was developed by William Lee Rand and other healers at The International Center for Reiki Training. Here is William's description of how this came about: "I received my Usui Reiki training in 1981 and 1982 while living in Hawaii. I became an Usui Reiki master in 1989 after moving to Michigan. After becoming a master, I decided to study with other Reiki masters so as to deepen my understanding of Reiki. I went on to take Reiki training from six other Usui masters including three from Japan. As I traveled around the country and to other countries teaching and practicing Reiki, I also made it a point to exchange sessions, information, attunements, and techniques with other Reiki masters and practitioners. I feel that healing is a never ending study and that ever greater benefits can come from the Higher Power if we seek them. Through the process of having studied with many Reiki masters I developed a deeper understanding of how the attunement processes, symbols and healing energies work.

I did not originally intend to create a new system of Reiki, but starting about 1989, I began being given non-Usui Reiki symbols and attunement techniques which were claimed to have benefit. I filed these symbols away along with the attunement processes that were included with them and also began experimenting with some of them. After a number of years, I had quite a collection and many of my students began asking me about these additional symbols wanting to know if they should use them. In the winter of 1993, I gathered together a number of my best students many of whom were spiritually sensitive, to experiment with the additional symbols, try them out and decide which were the most beneficial. We asked for guidance and through this process came up with a set of symbols that seemed to have the best energy. The symbols we chose had been channeled by several Reiki masters, including Marcy Miller, Kellie-Ray Marine, Pat Courtney, Catherine Mills Bellamont, and Marla Abraham. We also experimented with an attunement process to go with them. Later I was guided in the further development of the attunement process and this eventually evolved into a new system of Reiki.

Throughout the process, I prayed for help from the Higher Power and asked that I be connected to a healing energy that would be of greater benefit. In 1995, I was guided to more clearly define the system and to name it Karuna Reiki® which can be defined as the Reiki of Compassion. While some of the symbols in Karuna Reiki® are the same as those used by other schools and systems, because the attunements (now called Ignitions) are different and the intention is different, the energies that are connected to the Karuna Reiki® symbols are unique to the system."

The Holy Fire® aspect of this system was received 21 years later on January 23, 2014 and was added to both the ART/Master and the Karuna Reiki® systems. Holy Fire® II was added November 28, 2015 and Holy Fire® III was added September 21, 2018. The Holy Fire® energy refines and enhances the effectiveness of the Karuna healing energy and the energy of the Karuna symbols. In addition, the Holy Fire® symbol is the new master symbol for Karuna Reiki®. The next section explains Holy Fire® Reiki including what it is and where it came from.

Holy Fire®, A New Reiki Energy

Editors Note: This is a description of Holy Fire® Reiki when it first came out in January 2014. Since then, there have been a number of important changes and improvements. These include changing the word attunement to Placements and Ignitions, changing the pre-attunement to a regular Ignition for a total of four Ignitions, changing the name of the three-day ART/Master class to Reiki Master. This section was left in because it contains information on the history of Holy Fire® Reiki and also contains other relevant material. Please see page 20 for the latest improvements that have been made to Holy Fire® Reiki.

Holy Fire® came quickly and unexpectedly into my life as I was not seeking something as powerful and transformative as this. I first became aware of it and that I'd be teaching it on Thursday, January 23, 2014, which is just one day before I was to teach an ART/Master class. I was shown the symbol, received the attunement for it and how to give the attunements during three morning sessions I had with the late Janice Jones, a spiritual advisor I had been seeing regularly for the previous 19 years.

It was also explained to me that the Holy Fire® energy needed to connect to my system in a unique way and that this would require that the Tibetan symbols and the energy of the violet breath be retired. These energies had served their purpose and had helped me advance to this point and were also valuable in the healing they facilitated for others, but it was important that I let go of them. Once I gave my permission, the Holy Fire® energy came in and in a respectful way created the energetic changes necessary for this to take place. It was also explained that the Tibetan energies will remain appropriate and useful for those who have them and haven't taken the Holy Fire® Reiki training.

Of course all of this was a big surprise for me but the energy was so strong and the guidance so clear that I found it appropriate to accept the process and follow the instructions for teaching it.

The weekend before this class I taught a Reiki I&II class in which the Level II attunement and the healing energy we received was as powerful as a Karuna Reiki® attunement. I feel this must have been a preview and preparation for the Holy Fire®.

Pre-Attunement
On Friday I was guided to conduct a pre-attunement meditation prior to the ART attunement.[1] The pre-attunement meditation wasn't for the ART attunement, but for the Master attunement I was to give the next day for the Holy Fire® energy. I was guided to minimize the guidance I gave in the meditation and simply help the students move into a receptive state and let them go, allowing the Holy Fire® energy to take over and guide each one individually.

At that point I suggested that they trust in the light and allow it to guide their experience. Then I sat quietly meditating for 20 minutes or so and then suggested that each would return at a time that was right. Then once they were all back, I suggested that they write their experiences in their notebooks.

After this we shared our experiences and most students described a cleansing and purifying experience in which they felt they were being prepared to receive the Holy Fire®. They described having their chakras opened and purified and other kinds of purifying and some also described having spirits released with an understanding that they were no longer needed. This cleansing process continued after the meditation, and I was told that it would take about 24 hours for this process to be complete before each would be ready for the Master attunement, which is why it was done the day before.

[1] Please note that after Holy Fire® III, the pre-attunement which is also called the pre-Ignition is no longer used.

Master Attunement
The next day we did the Master attunement. This was done outdoors as had been the pre-attunement and ART attunement since the weather on Maui where the class was being held was warm and sunny.

Eleven students were sitting in a row. First I guided them in a focusing and vibration raising meditation. Then after a minute or so I said, "The attunement process will begin now. Remain with your eyes closed and your attention focused inwardly on your own inner experience. The attunement will guide itself, so allow yourself to be receptive and follow the guidance you receive." And that was all I did. I remained seated and did not physically interact with the students at all. I waited about 20 minutes and during this time I said prayers giving thanks for all the benefits each student was receiving. After this time, I suggested that each student return when the time was right and that after this, at their own pace, they were to write their experiences in their notebooks or otherwise allow an integration to take place. Then I stood up and returned to the Center and went to my room to relax and meditate.

When I heard the attunement music coming to an end, I came out to the classroom to find all the students seated in our classroom circle. They said that while the attunements were an individual experience, when each was complete, they all connected as one and as a group came back to the classroom together.

I asked people to share their thoughts about their experience. Each had his or her own inner experience but one student said that at the end and just after I had left, she asked that she be given a very definite physical sign so she would know that the attunement had taken place. At that point she and the others experienced a very strong and forceful wind that also contained strong spiritual energy. The wind came around them from behind and as they opened their eyes, they saw a small tornado-like wind encircle the chair I had been sitting in. The wind carried many leaves within its vortex and they were circling rapidly around the chair; then the chair shot straight up about 20 feet into the air and was spinning round very fast and then was blown across the yard about 100 feet away. While this was happening, the students, having just come out of a deep attunement experience, sat wide eyed as they watched this taking place. One student wanted to find out what the energy of the chair was like so she went to get it and said the chair was radiant with energy.

The attunement experiences students had contained similarities. The Holy Fire®, which burned very hot and was a multicolored flame, had installed itself in a space a few inches below the navel. Located near the place often referred to as the Dantian, I was told that this isn't the Dantian, but is near it and resonates on a much higher vibrational level. The flame purifies, and wherever it purifies it releases disharmonious energies, replacing those energies with the Holy Fire®. Some could see the flame; others could sense it in various ways. One student said it produced a hum-like sound that resembled the sound of Om, although not exactly the same, and that it gave him a sense of spiritual power. Others said it was like heat. Some said the flame surrounded their entire being. It was purifying but also healing and empowering. Many had a sense that all their worries for the future were gone and replaced with a sense that the Holy Fire® was preceding them into the future to take care of everything for them in a very healthy, peaceful and effective way. This produced a feeling of confidence that engendered the freedom to enjoy the present moment, knowing that everything was alright.

It is also apparent that the Holy Fire®, once ignited in the student, continues to grow in strength and vibration, cleansing more deeply and healing and empowering in ever more powerful ways. This feature gives a sense of profundity as we contemplate the experience of ever greater purification, healing and empowerment.

During the Reiki sessions when we practiced with the Holy Fire® symbol energy, some saw flames coming from the hands that seemed to flow throughout the client's entire being and often surrounded the client with a living flame. Feelings of deep peace and healing were expressed as we shared our experiences.

The introduction of the Holy Fire® experience into the teaching of the ICRT makes the attunements easier to do as there is no violet breath, no need to hold the Hui Yin or tongue and no use for the Tibetan symbols. Also, the Master attunement requires little for the Reiki Master to do as there is no physical interaction with the students, just a simple, short, guided meditation. The quality and nature of the energy also facilitates the teaching process and brings greater meaning to the experiences students have in class.

There is also a calm confidence in knowing that the Holy Fire® will guide and empower its own path forward to spread to all those who are willing to accept its blessings.

Experiences, Placements and Ignitions
Since our first experiences with Holy Fire® we have noted that the attunements for the Usui Master and Karuna levels are considerably different from what we have previously experienced. I have been told that because of this, they need a new name. We have been told to call them Ignitions. This is because the flame of the Holy Fire® is ignited in the student by a process that is conducted directly by the Holy Fire® energy. In Holy Fire® II, the Healing Attunement has been replaced with the Holy Fire® Healing Experience and the attunements for I&II and ART that were previously done have been replaced with Placements. These are conducted in a similar way as the Ignitions.

Experiences, Placements and Ignitions are done without the teacher physically interacting with the student. The teacher simply facilitates a short guided meditation to get the student into a receptive state of mind and then stops talking. At this point the Holy Fire® energy takes over, if it hasn't already done so and guides the student through the experience. The Holy Fire® provides the same benefits as attunements previously did such as giving the student the ability to use Reiki energy and empowers the symbols, or in the Master classes empowers the teacher to give Placements and Ignitions. An important difference is that the Holy Fire® comes directly from God and isn't limited by the lower vibration of the teacher. Because of this, the experiences provided are of a higher vibration, are more effective, create greater feelings of joy, peace, love, gratitude and so forth in the student.

Lineage
Holy Fire® has no lineage in the usual meaning of this word. Lineage as it is used with Reiki refers to the physical person who originally channeled the energy. No physical person originally did this. Therefore you can say that the lineage of Holy Fire® Reiki starts with God. Also, it is passed on directly by God to each student.

Registration for Teachers of Holy Fire®
A list of those who have taken Holy Fire® Reiki Master training has been set up that includes: Student name, city, state, country, class, date, teacher. This is a public list located at http://www.reikiwebstore.com/HolyFireStudentList.cfm. Proof of training is required to register and is required to buy manuals. Registration is free.

Privacy of the Symbol and Procedures
The Holy Fire® symbol and the Placement and Ignition procedures are similar to other Reiki symbols and procedures in that they are to be kept private and not shown to those who have not taken the Master training.

Holy Fire® Definition
The use of the word holy in the name Holy Fire® is not intended to have a religious meaning. The word holy has as its root meaning to be whole and complete and this is how it is used in Holy Fire® Reiki.[2] Therefore, Holy Fire® Reiki is a spiritual energy that creates wholeness through purification, healing, empowerment and guidance.

Only One Holy Fire® Master Class Required to Teach All Classes
If you have taken only Holy Fire® Karuna Reiki®, because you've received the Holy Fire® Ignitions, and you had previously taken ART/Master, you'll also be able to teach Holy Fire® ART/Master. And for the same reason, if you've taken Karuna Reiki® (the non-Holy Fire® version) and take Holy Fire® ART/Master, you'll be able to teach both Holy Fire® ART/Master and Holy Fire® Karuna Reiki®. Therefore you'll be able to teach Holy Fire® I&II, ART, Master and Karuna Master.

However, it is highly recommended that you take the Holy Fire® Master training you haven't received within the next year or so. This is recommended as taking the class will strengthen your understanding and improve your teaching skills; more importantly, the Holy Fire® energies and experiences are continually being upgraded and this will upgrade your Holy Fire® Reiki energies which will benefit you and your students.

---

[2] http://www.sciencechatforum.com/viewtopic.php?f=46&t=14247.

It is also apparent that the Holy Fire®, once ignited in the student, continues to grow in strength and vibration, cleansing more deeply and healing and empowering in ever more powerful ways. This feature gives a sense of profundity as we contemplate the experience of ever greater purification, healing and empowerment.

Holy Fire® Manuals
The Holy Fire® Karuna Reiki® and Usui/Holy Fire® Reiki Master manuals are available for purchase for those who have taken the training, who are registered and want to teach classes. The I&II manual can be used without changes as while the Holy Fire® symbol is used in the attunements, it is not given to the students.

Old Manuals
We will continue to sell the old manuals that contain the Tibetan symbols and violet breath for those who have not learned Holy Fire® Reiki.

Length of Holy Fire® Training
Some students who already have ART/Master or Karuna have asked if they could come by and get the ignitions to upgrade to Holy Fire®. Because of the nature of the training, this isn't possible. The Holy Fire® Reiki training needs to be done over a period of three days in either the Usui/Holy Fire® Reiki Master or Holy Fire® Karuna Reiki® training. This is the necessary time period, even for those who are already Usui and Karuna Reiki® Masters. There are several reasons for this. The number of ignitions that take place in Master classes has increased from what was previously done. There are four Holy Fire® ignitions which must be spread out over the three days. In addition, the Holy Fire® training creates a significant shift in the student's energy in which restrictive patterns are replaced with healthy energy by the Holy Fire®. This shift takes time and also needs to be done in a supportive environment in the presence of the teacher and other students.

Learning Holy Fire® Reiki
Holy Fire® Reiki is taught by ICRT Licensed Reiki Master Teachers (LRMTs). You can also learn from any registered Holy Fire® Reiki teacher. A list of LRMT classes and a list of registered teachers can be found at www.reiki.org.

Healing Religious Trauma
Holy Fire® Reiki uses some concepts that are also used in religion. These concepts are God, Holy Spirit and Jesus. However, Holy Fire® Reiki does not use these concepts in a religious context. It is important to keep in mind that religion doesn't own the sole use of these terms. These spiritual resources existed long before religion, and there is no requirement that one be part of a religious practice in order to have access to them.

It is our perception, understanding and experience that it is possible to have a developing relationship with God, Holy Spirit and Jesus without being part of a religious practice. However, people who have experienced a Christian upbringing will often decide to stop going to church because of the dislike they have toward the fear, shame, and condemnation to which it exposes them.[3] Also, they often stop using the word God and instead use words like Source or Creator or Universal Spirit or something similar. While there may be some value in choosing to use different words, doing so will not remove the unresolved trauma. Rather than using different words, it is much better to heal the trauma one has toward these terms so that one can use them freely and openly if one chooses to do so; as long as the trauma goes unhealed, it will weaken one's connection to these spiritual resources regardless of the name one uses to describe them.

One of the significant benefits of Holy Fire® Reiki is its ability to heal religious trauma; this healing energy has a frequency high enough to locate and heal any religious trauma one may have experienced. As this happens, one's connection to the source of Reiki strengthens. Also, when religious trauma heals, it brings new feelings of freedom and openness in which one can easily accept the religion of one's parents as a choice they have the right to make. It will also allow you to enter a church or see a car go by with a religious bumper sticker without feeling uncomfortable or experiencing religious prejudice. As you heal your ability to accept the spiritual choices of others, you heal your ability to freely choose the spiritual path that feels right for you.

So, if you feel uncomfortable that the manual uses the words God, Holy Spirit and Jesus, keep in mind that what is most likely happening is that old, unresolved emotional distress involving religious trauma is being brought to the surface to more easily heal and release. It is incredible the extent that Holy Fire® Reiki can provide this type of healing; the freedom and clarity it gives you will allow you to accept and connect with people lovingly regardless of their religious background.

While we honor the choices people have made concerning whether to be part of a religious practice, Holy Fire® Reiki isn't religious, yet, at the same time, it helps one heal the harm one may have experienced because of being raised in a religious environment.

Teaching Other Styles of Reiki
If a student is already teaching another style of Reiki other than Holy Fire® and feels guided to continue to do so, they will be able to do this. The issue is that some of the other systems of Reiki are not entirely in harmony with Holy Fire® Reiki and because of this, could reduce the effectiveness of one's Holy Fire® Reiki if one were to continue teaching them. However, a new feature of Holy Fire® III is that it now has the ability to harmonize any other system of Reiki one may already be teaching with Holy Fire® Reiki. After taking this class, if one wants to teach the other system, all that is necessary is to say a short prayer, asking that Jesus or the Holy Fire® or both will work out any incompatibilities in the energies so that the systems can work in harmony. Then follow your guidance in terms of when this process has completed.

---

[3] This may also be true for those who have received religious training from other religions besides Christianity.

Holy Fire® Reiki Can Be a Spiritual Path
This style of Reiki has unlimited potential in terms of healing your issues and developing your spiritual nature. It works directly with your Spirit and because of this has the potential of developing higher levels of consciousness within you. This includes developing the qualities of joy, peace, love, compassion, the ability to forgive others and yourself, becoming non-judgmental and creating a tremendous feeling of spiritual freedom and happiness. Those who have followed this path, have found it to open up into an amazing opportunity for the continual unfoldment of all the qualities that are healthy for a person to have.

Description of Holy Fire® Reiki

Holy Fire® Reiki which was introduced by the ICRT in January 2014 is a new form of Reiki. It is both powerful and gentle and provides purification, healing, empowerment and guidance. It is included as part of our Usui Reiki classes and has also been added to Karuna Reiki® training.

The Holy Fire® energy is noticeably more refined and comes from a higher level of consciousness. Some of the qualities students have experienced include:

- Works continuously even when not thinking about it and spontaneously heals issues as they come up.
- Always respects free will.
- Heals deeply and quickly without distress.
- Heals relationships and interactions with others.
- Releases worry and replaces it with a sense of safety in a most pronounced way.
- Spontaneously provides guidance that is palatable for every level of life experience.
- Tends to develop all the personality traits that are healthy for a person to have such as love of self and others, kindness, patience, confidence, vitality, enthusiasm, optimism, trust, joy, peace and so forth.
- One of the more wonderful effects is a feeling of being loved. This is a deep and refined nurturing feeling.
- Once received, it continues to develop itself to be more evolved and effective.

These qualities are present in I&II and become more pronounced in the Reiki Master and Karuna classes.

Birth of Holy Fire® II

Placements instead of Attunements
In September, 2015, I was contemplating the way Holy Fire® was taught; we had regular hands on attunements for levels I, II and ART and used the hands off style Ignition process for the Master level. I understood the Ignition style was more powerful because of the fact that the teacher's energy was not involved. I wondered if it would be possible to give an Ignition type process for levels I&II and ART so I asked Jesus this question during a session with Janice Jones. Jesus said yes, it is possible and that he had been preparing me to be able to receive this ability. He then gave me the ability to do this during an Ignition like experience and explained how to do Placements for levels I, II and ART and how to pass this ability on to my Master students.

I taught my first I&II class using the Placement method at the end of November, 2015 and also taught this new style in the ART/Master and Karuna classes that followed. The Placements proved to be even more effective than the attunements and the Holy Fire® energy in all the classes was upgraded! After this, I created a Holy Fire® II upgrade class which I taught to our Licensed Teachers and also provided it to the other Holy Fire® students in two live webinars. (The webinar recording continues to be available to all Holy Fire® students who would like to receive the upgrade. Find it listed in my Reiki class schedule.)

Healing in the River of Life Experience
In addition, I received many additional sessions so that I would be able to pass the ability to give Placements on to others in the Master classes. This process was called the Healing in the River of Life Experience, which is conducted in the Holy Fire® II Master classes. It not only passes on the ability to give Placements if the student doesn't already have it, it also passes on the ability to conduct the Healing in the River of Life Experience.

Holy Fire® Healing Experience
In Holy Fire® II, the Healing Attunement is transformed into the Holy Fire® Healing Experience and the ability to conduct this experience is given to the student in class during the Healing in the River of Life Experience. The prep for this Experience is done the same way that it was done for the Healing Attunement.

The Experience of Holy Fire® II
After teaching the new Holy Fire® II system and talking with my students I gained a clearer understanding of how the Placements work and their results. Students who were reviewing the class and had already received the attunements for the class reported that the Placements produce what appears to be a different Reiki energy than what was received in Usui Reiki. The energy is brighter, provides a more uplifting experience and is a more effective healing energy. In addition, when received in a Master class, the ability to give Holy Fire® II attunements is released completely and replaced with the ability to give Placements.

Introduction to Holy Fire® III Reiki

Holy Fire® Reiki Overview

Holy Fire® Reiki is a type of Reiki energy and a system of Reiki healing based on Holy Fire® energy. Mentioned in the Bible, Holy Fire® energy has been active in the world since ancient times. Based on sessions with the late Janice Jones, a spiritual adviser, our understanding is that God, working through the Holy Spirit created Holy Fire® energy and Jesus is able to access and use this energy and also provide it to others. While the words, *Jesus, God,* and *Holy Spirit* are used by religion, in the practice of Holy Fire® Reiki we do not consider them to be religious, but instead, consider them to be spiritual in nature. Furthermore, we think of Jesus as a spiritual master rather than as a religious figure. Our understanding of these topics is based mainly on direct spiritual perception and on the healing benefits this energy provides and that have been experienced by hundreds of Reiki practitioners and teachers. Greater clarity concerning this information has come to us after experiencing a process that involved the healing of religious trauma; please see page 16.

It is important to keep in mind that the entire Holy Fire® Reiki system is not something I designed or created, but something that came to me as part of healing sessions I had with two talented spiritual healers who channeled illumined beings.

While Jesus was the spiritual master who introduced Holy Fire® Reiki, he is also part of a group called the Brothers and Sisters of the Light. This group is a combined force of all illumined beings and includes those beings from which all the world's religions and spiritual paths have originated. Previously they were in the formless world but came into the world of form so they could assist us in the development, teaching and use of Holy Fire® Reiki.

Its expression as a Reiki healing system moves Holy Fire® energy from being an experience that has happened occasionally in the past to those fortunate enough to experience it, to be an energy anyone initiated as a Holy Fire® Reiki Master can utilize regularly. This training takes place in the Usui/Holy Fire® Master and Holy Fire® Karuna Reiki® Master courses. The energy is also present in the Usui/Holy Fire® versions of Reiki I and II.

I first experienced Holy Fire® Reiki energy on January 23, 2014, when Janice Jones channeled the energy from Jesus. I presented it to my Reiki Master class a few days later, and the students indicated that they experienced it to be stronger healing energy and guided by a higher level of consciousness than any of them had previously experienced.

Our Licensed Reiki Master Teachers (LRMTs) received the ability to use this energy during attunements with myself and directly in sessions with Janice Jones. They also agreed that there was a perceptible improvement in the quality and strength of their Reiki energy. Each began using this energy in sessions and teaching it to students. At that point, the energy was part of the attunement process for the Master level only. Subsequently, the word *attunement* changed to *Ignition* as it appeared that the flame of the Holy Fire® energy ignited within the student during the attunement.

In December 2015, through instruction by Jesus received through Janice Jones, the system gained the ability to use this energy during Reiki I and II attunements. Because each student appeared to have the energy placed within them, the term for this process changed from *attunement* to *Placement*. At this point, we noted that the overall effectiveness of the Holy Fire® energy had increased for all levels of instruction; because of this, we called the system Holy Fire® II.

Holy Fire® III
During spiritual healing sessions with Colleen Benelli, one of our LRMTs who has extensive training in shamanism and who also received training from Janice, I received information that something new was coming to my Reiki practice, although there was no description as to its nature. Also, when contemplating the Reiki classes I would conduct at Mount Kurama in Japan, the sacred mountain where Usui Sensei had a spiritual experience and received the gift of Reiki, I became aware that something particularly important would take place there.

Then on September 21, 2018, while conducting those classes, a new level of Holy Fire® energy appeared. Colleen provided guidance from Jesus that I was to teach these classes differently. Instead of giving a pre-Ignition as before in the Holy Fire® II classes, I was to change it to a regular Ignition for a total of four Ignitions rather than the original three as was previously done.

The teacher conducts an Ignition by providing a short, guided meditation lasting five to seven minutes or so and then stops talking while gentle music plays in the background. This process allows the Ignition energy to interact directly with the student's energy field rather than being channeled through the teacher. The whole experience continues for about 26 minutes altogether. After I conducted the guided meditation for the first Ignition, and while sitting there allowing the process to proceed for the students without my interaction, I experienced something profound.

I inwardly observed a tube of translucent white light which had stars moving up through it. Then I saw that this tube was coming from a ball of translucent white light within myself. I also saw an arc of light coming from the surface of the ball of light, and I felt the spiritual power the ball of light contained. Then I was invited to enter the ball of light and when I did, I initially experienced pain. But, the light said to let go, as this was just my Culturally-Created Self releasing. When I let go, the pain disappeared, and I felt peace and a great depth of spiritual power. At that point, I said to myself, "I am Free, I am Free, Forevermore, I am Free." This was one of the most powerful spiritual experiences I have had.

When this was happening, I also observed that the three Holy Fire® flames installed during my first Holy Fire® training—one below the navel, one above the head and one in the heart—were joined together by a shaft of light. Then eventually, they expanded and filled my entire physical body. The effects of this experience lasted for a week or so during which I traveled to Taiwan and taught an Usui/Holy Fire® III Master class. Slowly the energy seemed to subside, then at the end of October, while teaching, it ramped up again then again subsided. However, these experiences left a residual effect, and I could tell they were conditioning my system to adjust to higher spiritual energies which will stay steadily present. I was also told that these "peak" experiences would continue.

As of May 2019, I have taught 23 Holy Fire® III classes. Some of my students and our LRMTs who upgraded to Holy Fire® III have also taught classes. So far, there are about 600 students who have received the Holy Fire® III energy. Many of these students have been Reiki Masters for years and have extensive experience taking Reiki classes, teaching and giving sessions. The effects of the energy reported by these students and those of the other teachers are consistent. All people indicate that this Reiki energy is more effective, and those who had Holy Fire® II report that Holy Fire® III is a definite improvement over what they previously had. Many report that the energy feels both subtle and more powerful and that new healing is taking place, often on an extraordinary level.

As we have experienced Holy Fire® III, a new set of concepts given to us explain the energy and the levels of healing that are taking place. The following describes the main ideas.

The Authentic Self
Within each person resides a compelling and extraordinary aspect of our inner nature that is composed of the pure, unaltered self. This part connects directly to God consciousness and possesses the awareness and power of the Universe. It is unlimited in its ability to know and to do, and it is who we really are. (Note that psychology also uses the term "Authentic Self" and while there is some similarity, our definition has significant differences.)

The energy of the Holy Fire® III Reiki class ignites and reveals the light of the Authentic Self, making it easier for a person to see and experience. Students find that their light, their wholeness and brilliance, is right there inside them. To some, the view of their Authentic Self has appeared as a beautiful light within; as brilliant as the sun. The remarkable qualities of their soul, life purpose and their inner truth become revealed to them, and also, they feel they are now empowered to fulfill their life purpose!

The influx of Holy Fire® III energy is a unique experience that feels safe, steady and grounded. Rather than being aware of one's Authentic Self in an altered state, or as something happening in a high and distant place, it is experienced as being present within one's physical body and as part of one's everyday life.

One's personality, ego, emotions and thoughts rise to a higher level of consciousness so that one can view life with heightened awareness and enjoyment. Innovation, intuition, inventiveness, creativity and solutions are more readily available and expressed in one's intentions, goals, decisions and actions.

After the process makes the Authentic Self visible to one's inner awareness, the process continues to develop and further highlight its attributes. These include qualities such as intellect, talents, identity, authority and voice, and spirituality, personality and more.

Unfortunately, most people have little connection to their Authentic Self. One of the reasons for this is the development of, and identification with, the Culturally-Created Self.

The Culturally-Created Self

When a person is born, he or she is dependent on his or her parents for food, shelter, clothing and physical contact; everything necessary to support the life of the child. This dependence creates a strong relationship between the child and its parents and forms the basis for the development of the child's identity. The influence of the parents also teaches the child what is important in life and what is not.

While the young child usually has some awareness of the Authentic Self, the parents often discourage its expression because they do not have contact with nor understand their own Authentic Selves. Because of the influence of the parents and exposure to the everyday world around it, the child is encouraged to develop a personality based on cultural conditioning. So, as the child grows and matures, he or she comes to identify more completely with the Culturally-Created Self. As this happens, awareness of the Authentic Self fades until in many people there is little or no awareness of it at all. The Culturally-Created Self has a limited view of who it is and what it can accomplish, and by comparison to the Authentic Self, possesses greatly diminished awareness.

Origin of Dormant Unhealed Energy

As a child grows into adulthood, it often becomes clear to him or her that they exhibit behaviors that are not considered acceptable by adults. These behaviors can include angry shouting and screaming, crying, pouting, fearful shaking and so forth. Insecurity, anger, jealousy, impatience, selfishness, fear, sadness or other similar feelings are often a cause of these behaviors. If parents do not show the child how to handle these feelings healthily, and instead as is often the case, tell the child, "Stop that!" or "Don't act that way!" over time, the child learns to push these feelings inside and hold them in place, and they go unexpressed.

Also, many times when children suppress their feelings, they are rewarded by the parents telling them, "Good girl!" or "Good boy!" or they hear their parents tell other adults to look at what a good boy or a good girl he or she is, or other similar words. These actions reinforce the child's behavior of hiding feelings and encourage the child to deny that they have such feelings at all. Eventually, as this process develops, these "unwanted" feelings begin to be held inside automatically by conditioning that takes place in the subconscious mind and because of this, they are unexpressed.

This pattern of behavior can develop to the point where the person does not know they have these feelings. Because these feelings are unknown, the person no longer gives them energy, and instead directs their awareness toward what society considers positive qualities and develops the expression of those feelings instead. When unhealthy emotions do not receive energy or attention, over time, they become dormant.

Also, the unhealed dormant parts reduce a person's ability to experience feelings and emotions and reduce the ability to respond effectively to the challenges of life. A person becomes less flexible and is not as creative in their ability to solve problems, in being productive, or in finding enjoyment in life. In other words, the unhealed dormant parts limit the person's ability to enjoy the full range of strong, positive feelings they would otherwise experience.

Because a person isn't aware of the unhealed dormant parts, they are not motivated to heal them. Also, these parts are unusually challenging to heal, and up to this point, regular Reiki energy or other healing methods have difficulty discovering them, and so they rarely heal.

These unhealed dormant parts build up in layers that cover up the Authentic Self and often create a thick hard shell that prevents the Authentic Self from being known to the person or expressing its amazing potential. Experiences from this lifetime and past lives, ancestral history and cellular memory, to name a few, can cause the buildup of unhealed dormant layers that block our Authentic Self from being seen and so stop it from contributing to the quality of our lives. The unhealed dormant parts present a significant challenge to our healing process. However, there is a solution.

Holy Fire® III Heals Dormant Unhealed Parts

Holy Fire® III Reiki originates from higher dimensions of consciousness we call the heavens. In the fourth and fifth heavens, the levels of consciousness there are aware of the dormant parts and can heal them, and as healing happens, more of the Authentic Self can emerge. As this occurs, an increasing level of serenity, vitality and joy expresses itself, accompanied by an awareness that this is who you *really* are.

Joining People Together

Holy Fire® III contains the fire of unity. Its purpose is to unify all people. As one becomes ever more aware of the Authentic Self and begins to assume it as one's identity, it becomes clear that everyone has an Authentic Self within them and because of this, we can easily see we are all one. The awareness that we are all one makes it easy to accept others regardless of the diversity of race, religion or beliefs, national origin, gender, sexual orientation or age. In this way, we can more easily work in harmony with all people to create peace and happiness in the world.

Interestingly, the promotion of this process is the purpose of the World Peace Crystal Grids placed at the North Pole in 1997, the South Pole in 1999 and the Old City of Jerusalem in 2004. There are also grids at the ICRT Center in Michigan and the ICRT Center on Maui. Previous issues of *Reiki News Magazine*, and our website at www.reiki.org, describe them in greater detail. The inscription on the Peace Grids reads, *May the followers of all religions, and spiritual paths work together to create peace among all people on Earth.* This proclamation, also embedded in the energy of Holy Fire® III, has already started to influence the people of our planet and is destined to bring what so many have prayed for and worked to create for thousands of years—peace on earth.

Location of Holy Fire® III Energy
In the Holy Fire® and Holy Fire® II Master classes, the energy consisted of three spiritual flames; one below the navel, one above the head and one in the heart. In the Holy Fire® III Master class, if one already has Holy Fire®, a shaft of light first joins the three flames together and then the energy spreads throughout the entire body sometimes appearing as thousands of small flames. This action takes place gradually over a period of weeks or a month or more. If one has not previously taken a Holy Fire® Reiki Master class and takes the Holy Fire® III Master class, the energy will simply spread as small flames throughout the entire body. As this happens, it grounds the experience in the present time and the material world, making the experience feel very real and a normal part of the person's experience.

Purpose of the Holy Fire® Flames
The Holy Fire® flames act as transformers that allow the Holy Fire® energy to come from the formless realm and express in the world of form including expression in the material world. However, as a person progresses in the ability to assimilate higher states of consciousness, a point is reached in which the person's inner nature can work with the energy of the formless realm directly. When this happens, the Holy Fire® flames are no longer necessary and cease to be part of the person's Holy Fire® experience.

Healing the Ego
The ego is the part of ourselves associated with our identity and sense of self. It is who we know ourselves to be. The ego makes use of inner resources such as memory as well as feelings and emotions, all of which play a vital role in the learning process. It also uses logic and intuition and through the physical senses, gains awareness of the outer world. Also, and most importantly, the inner senses make possible the awareness of higher states of consciousness and other resources that can be used to shape our lives.

Our understanding of the ego is affected by the beliefs we have about it which often come from society. If we believe, as our society often indicates, that the ego can be a problem and is to be ignored, then this affects how we perceive the ego. This concept is also part of the information expressed in much of the literature about spiritual development which similarly suggests that the ego is what we must eliminate or otherwise set aside if we are to progress on the spiritual path.

If we believe the ego is a problem and is what is holding us back on our spiritual path, then this is how we perceive and relate to the ego. When we do this, it is difficult to understand and make use of the value the ego provides for our lives and for our ability to evolve and connect with higher levels of consciousness.

However, what society and the spiritual community are focused on, as portrayed above, is not the ego in its entirety, but the unhealed ego. It is the unhealed ego which produces the unhealthy tendencies about which people are concerned. It is essential to realize that if something is, in fact, unhealed, then we must accept that it can be healed. This acceptance is especially true for those of us who are healers.

However, the ability of the ego to heal is an important concept that is often overlooked because society, as well as many of the spiritual traditions, have not had effective methods to heal the ego. Because of this, the usual method of dealing with the ego is to set it to the side and to ignore it and attempt to create an outward expression that is devoid of the ego. This method is difficult to do and often results in choosing a spiritual path in which one lives an isolated life, living in a cave or cloistered from society in a monastery or in some other way separated from society and attempting to disconnect from much of the material world.

An important discovery we have made about Holy Fire® III energy is that it does have the ability to heal the ego which is a genuinely exciting discovery because once the ego begins to heal, the positive qualities of the ego begin to reveal themselves. As this takes place, it allows us to make use of the wonderful qualities and potentials the ego possesses.

One aspect revealed to us is that the ego's true purpose is to be an expression of our divine nature on earth and to help us accomplish our spiritual purpose in the material world. It also has access to special healing abilities and higher states of consciousness we can enjoy right now. But, to experience these beautiful gifts, we must let go of any negative ideas we may have about the ego; as we do this, it will reveal the beauty and wonder that resides within. The energy of Holy Fire® III can help us do this by healing the ego and creating a stronger connection to our Authentic Self.

All heavens and higher states of consciousness are within the physical body now, and their purpose is to express through the physical body here on earth. Some awareness of the resources in each heaven exists in most people, but the potential that resides in each level is much greater than what most are aware. Holy Fire® III increases our awareness of these levels of consciousness and quickens our ability to make use of their resources. After a student receives the Holy Fire® energy as part of a Master class, this awareness becomes part of a developmental process that unfolds over time and in ways that are different for each person. Also, the speed at which the revelation of the heavens takes place can also change as time goes by, speeding up during times of healing and personal development, and slowing down during periods of stability. However, the increased awareness and development that one experiences will remain available and be added to additional improvements as they come along.

Editor's Note: Parts of the above section first appeared in the Winter, 2018 and Spring, 2019 issues of *Reiki News Magazine*.

The Twelve Heavens

This is a more nuanced understanding of metaphysical energies and is based on the experience of those who have a more sensitive awareness of higher dimensional consciousness. It provides a better understanding of the various kinds of energy that are around us so we can choose which energies are compatible and supportive of our healing and development. This concept has been expressed by others using different metaphors and descriptive methods such as three levels of consciousness or the 2nd level being described as the astral plane.

First Heaven
This is the atmosphere that surrounds the physical Earth including the air, the clouds and rain as well as all the living things in the atmosphere such as the birds and insects and so forth. It also includes the Earth herself and all the people and living things on the planet. The first heaven is where we live. In the first heaven, there are people who have good intentions and want to help others, and there are people who want to take advantage of others.In fact, most people here have at least some portion of their ego that needs to heal and usually have a combination of healthy and unhealthy energies, values and intentions.

Second Heaven
This is a field of consciousness similar to the first heaven, except it is non-physical. It contains spirit beings, energies, thought forms, concepts and so forth. Most of the beings here have unhealed egos. Even so, some of these beings are on a spiritual path in which they are seeking to heal their egos and become a pure expression of their Authentic Selves. But in a similar way as in the material world, most of the beings here are not doing this, but are simply attempting to use the resources and possibilities that exist within the second heaven based on the motivations of their unhealed egos.

The second heaven is also where the spirits reside that are mentioned in the section about Healing Spirit Attachments on page 53. These spirits attempt to take advantage of people in the material world and also are competitive in this way with the other spirits in the second heaven. They usually have hidden agendas and try to appear to have a high vibration when they actually have a low vibration. Some attempt to appear to be enlightened or to have other "gifts" they use to entice people. You can tell when a person is being influenced by second heaven spirits if they act as if they are superior to others because of the "special" benefits they receive from spirit guides they work with. While it is important to know that these spirits can provide some help, it is of a much lower vibration than what comes from beings in the third heaven or higher. One of the unfortunate aspects of these spirits is that they often try to violate free will; in effect they are con artists and try to convince people to trust them when they actually have a selfish agenda that they hide from the people they work with. However, do not worry about these beings as the Holy Fire® energy you are receiving in this class will easily protect you from them.

It is also important to know that the second heaven contains spirits who are part of The Brothers and Sisters of the Light. While these spirits are not from the second heaven, they have positioned themselves in the second heaven to help the spirits on this level and to create a path to allow these spirits to move up into the higher heavens if they choose to do so. They are also here to help those of us in the material world to easily move beyond this level and rise up into to the beautiful levels of consciousness that are beyond the second heaven.

Third Heaven
The third heaven and higher is where it is possible to completely heal the ego and become a pure expression of God's love, awareness and power. The beings and energies here have an open-hearted love for everyone and everything. They are connected with unlimited energy, joy, peace, and happiness; everything good. The energy of this heaven is entirely healthy, uplifting, joyful, caring, loving, peaceful, trustworthy, and life supporting. And the third heaven energies can be very powerful, able to overcome any difficulty that has been created by second heaven energies or beings, and to purify, heal, and empower in meaningful ways. It is the purpose of this energy and consciousness of the third heaven to connect directly to the first heaven and bring the third heaven benefits directly to the people of the Earth. One of the features of the third heaven is that the energies and beings always respect free will. And while they want to help us, they cannot do so unless we accept their offer of help.

In addition, in order to benefit from the third heaven, we must be willing to release ourselves from the influences of the second heaven. It will not really work very well for us to have a combination of second and third heaven energies as the second heaven energies will always lower our vibration and limit the benefits the third heaven can provide. However, this is a process the third heaven energies are able to assist us with and is expressed in the purification phase of the Holy Fire® experience.

Fourth Heaven
The fourth heaven provides additional healing in preparation for entering the fifth heaven. This healing includes awareness of and trust in the idea that a higher way of living life is possible involving the release of unhealthy competitiveness, acceptance of higher guidance and the gift of wonderful new energies that heal and empower you.

Fifth Heaven
When revealed, the energy of the fifth heaven begins a continuing process of leading the dormant self in the direction of complete healing and allowing the Authentic Self to replace the Culturally-Created Self. This process takes place at a pace that varies with each person but can feel remarkably fast, yet smooth and stable.

In class, during an Ignition, often the Authentic Self can become visible to one's inner awareness, and one may be invited to enter the Authentic Self. This occurrence causes the Culturally-Created Self to begin a releasing process which can be an extraordinary experience.

Even though with this process a person becomes connected to and works from the higher heavens, they are still very much present in their physical body. As the energy from the heavens enters the physical body, the health and well-being of the body increases, making it more comfortable to be in the body, enabling one to deal more successfully with life, helping solve any issues one might encounter and helping one make use of opportunities as they arise.

Sixth Heaven
On this level, the intellect begins a healing process. Rather than having an attitude that the ideas and knowledge one possesses makes one better than others, they begin being valued for how they can be used to improve the quality of one's life and the lives of others including family members and society in general. In addition, a love of learning and of knowledge and its application to everyday life can develop.

Improvements in communication can also take place. This involves a more thoughtful choice of words making it more enjoyable for others to listen to what you have to say. Your words may also spontaneously begin to be combined with the Holy Fire® III energy making what you say feel soothing and even providing a noticeable level of healing for those you speak with. Writing can be affected in a similar way.

In addition, one may develop an interest in acquiring a greater depth of understanding in topics one has previously had an interest in and also develop interest in studying new subjects. This could expand into learning to play a musical instrument, taking singing or dancing lessons, beginning an exercise program, getting involved in a new hobby, learning to play new games, writing poetry or articles for a magazine or writing a book, learning a foreign language, taking a trip to a foreign country, taking college classes and so forth.

> **The Holy Fire® III system of healing increases one's quality of consciousness at the same time it provides an extraordinary healing experience.**

Seventh Heaven
This level deals with healing the ego. In many spiritual and metaphysical systems, it is taught that the ego is the enemy and that it must be negated or overcome, or even killed; or otherwise, one must rise above the ego if one is to proceed forward on one's spiritual path. It is important to note that from our observation, what is being focused on here isn't the ego, but the unhealed ego. And for some unknown reason, even though healing is often part of spiritual and metaphysical studies, little is said about the possibility of healing the ego. However, the guidance we have been given through Holy Fire® III is that while the unhealed ego can be an impediment to one's spiritual development, the unhealed ego can be healed! And once healed, it is no longer an impediment, but is able to fulfill a very important purpose. The healed ego is a vehicle for the expression of higher consciousness in the material world!

This is a remarkable idea that we had not heard before, yet, based on the experiences of those who have taken Holy Fire® III classes, it is apparent that many receive this important gift. In addition, while it is rare, there is at least one other spiritual school that has this teaching as well. Google "healed ego" and you'll see what I mean.

If our purpose is to bring spiritual values to the material world, then this can be more effectively done through a healed ego. Holy Fire® III contains the energy needed to heal the ego. This healing process happens at a pace that is right for each student and happens spontaneously without the student needing to do anything special except use Holy Fire® Reiki with themselves and others. As this happens, one begins to experience higher levels of consciousness becoming grounded in one's physical body. One also begins to have a greater awareness of higher consciousness in the material world and in everyday life.

As the ego heals, one becomes less and less upset by those who are on "ego trips" and it becomes easy and natural to deal with them in a relaxed and healthy way. Often when a person is on an "ego trip," it isn't what they say that can be off putting, but how they say it. But as your ego heals, it is easy to hear the factual and often helpful part of the information they are communicating and then understand and make use of it in a healthy way. Doing this will also help the person on the "ego trip" to realign to a more all-inclusive state of mind. Overall, with Holy Fire® III, the material world comes to be experienced as a safer, healthier and more enjoyable place to be.

Searching for spirituality in a place that is disconnected from the material world can result in one becoming detached from one's physical needs and responsibilities. This makes the process of healing our planet more difficult by encouraging an attitude of one not wanting to be here. Being able to connect with a spiritual energy that is able to express itself in the material world is a powerful solution; it encourages us to be fully present and empowers us to make a difference in the world we live in.

The healed ego is a vehicle for the expression of higher consciousness in the material world!

Eighth Heaven
It is on this level that we begin to appreciate more deeply the fact that we are self-aware and that this is a tremendous gift. Gratitude for this gift develops, opening one's awareness more fully and preparing us for the ninth heaven. As this happens, restrictions we have unknowingly placed on ourselves become known to us as illusions and fly away, disappearing into nothingness. Holy Fire® III empowers this process, opening a clear space all around us in which we experience a lightness of being.

Ninth Heaven
This level is where a person begins to be aware of their human/divine nature. It becomes clearly understood and experienced that the physical body is the spiritual home of our divine consciousness. This process is a unification in which what once seemed

separate becomes lovingly compatible and harmoniously joined together. This merging results in a feeling that all is right within oneself and within everything around you.

Tenth Heaven
This level is a continuation and development of the previous level in which you realize more completely that your divine nature is part of your human nature. The human and divine natures become more aware of each other and begin working together in greater harmony. This awareness results in one's life energy becoming guided more directly by divine consciousness.

Eleventh Heaven
On this level, the awareness of essential skills and abilities that are needed to fulfill one's life purpose begin to be understood. This realization leads to one being motivated to acquire and develop these personal resources.

Twelfth Heaven
It is from this level of consciousness that people gain an understanding of their purpose on earth. It is also the level in which an individual decides what type of consciousness and kinds of personal energy and knowledge they will need on their earthly path. At this stage of unfoldment, our divine consciousness becomes more fully embodied and begins to manifest the fulfillment of our life purpose. It does this by opening a pathway into the future in which any obstacles that may have slowed or blocked our journey are healed and released before we experience them; this creates feelings of trust and confidence and a natural feeling of acceptance that one will be successful.

As one proceeds along this path, any feelings that have previously caused worry and concern, and a state of vigilance in preparation to ward off opposition to one's life, are transformed into a state of heightened perception. In this state, there is awareness of the heavens, and knowledge within one's core that the forces of the universe are rising up to support and fulfill one's reason for being. This allows one to relax and feel safe.

The Formless Realm

The Formless Realm is an area of pure consciousness located above the heavens. All beings in this realm are in a state of pure bliss. In metaphysics, it is thought that it is out of this realm that the world of form originates.[4] The name of the Distant symbol, written in Japanese kanji, embodies this concept. This kanji is from a Japanese Zen Buddhist mantra which means: "The origin of all is pure consciousness."

It is interesting to note that this understanding about how everything that exists originated out of the formless realm has a parallel in the science of astrophysics. When scientists contemplate the origin of the Universe, they refer to the Big Bang.

---

[4] https://en.wikipedia.org/wiki/Buddhist_cosmology. Note that both the formless world and the world of form referred to here are in the non-material, spiritual realms.

Time and space along with energy and matter and the known and unknown laws of physics and chemistry—in other words, everything that exists—originated from the Big Bang. According to this theory, the Big Bang originated out of a singularity which is a point with no dimension. When asked what the origin of the singularity is, astrophysicists say that since everything that exists came from the singularity, the singularity came into existence out of nothing.[5]

The Brothers and Sisters of the Light

At the beginning of 2018, when we were receiving additional information about the development of Holy Fire® energy, one day I noticed that Jesus was sitting on my right side. He was there to inspire and guide me as he had been doing, but this time I also saw a presence on my left side. When I asked who this was, they told me, "We are the Brothers and Sisters of the Light." The energy around this group felt extraordinary, and I wanted to know more.

In my next session with Colleen Benelli, we learned a great deal about who they were and why they are here. They said that they had been in the formless realm but realized that we needed help developing the Holy Fire® energy, and to do this they entered the world of form so they could interact with us in the material world. To align more closely with human energy, they also took on gender. Later I learned that part of their consciousness remained in the formless realm and part in the world of form and by doing this they can bring the consciousness of the formless realm into the material world. This group is composed of the founders of all the world's religions and spiritual paths and is also known as the Ascended Masters.

When each was in the material world, the religions and spiritual paths they created were mostly separate from each other. However, when one goes up into higher states of consciousness, one gets to a place where the spirits of all the founders have merged and have become one. This oneness is an important concept as it explains in greater detail why all religions and spiritual paths have the same origin and that their founders have become one with each other on higher levels of awareness.

Unification Consciousness
As one more fully grasps this concept and feels this oneness, when meeting members of different religions and spiritual paths, one can more easily find rapport with those individuals, for through Holy Fire® Reiki one connects directly to the founders of each person's religion. This connection brings a feeling of recognition and a sense of brother/sisterhood with the person. It is a method of not just having a peaceful acceptance of all religions and spiritual paths, but of feeling spiritually connected with them. This state provides a deep release of tension in one's psyche and is wonderful to experience.

This connection is one of the purest qualities of Holy Fire® III as it unifies our divine nature with our human nature and makes us aware that divine light fills everything

---

[5] https://en.wikipedia.org/wiki/A_Universe_from_Nothing

in our everyday lives. It also enables us to see that the divine light inside ourselves is also inside everyone. They tell us that this experience is called Unification Consciousness and is a state shared by the Brothers and Sisters of the Light which they also share with all those who contact them.

The Unification Consciousness which is within each person also has a collective intention for humanity which is to love ourselves and each other along with all life on earth. One truth is that we need not wait for everyone to have this realization but can experience it for ourselves right now, and when we do, our lives enter this beautiful state immediately! By allowing this to happen, we make it easier for others to enter this state also.

Becoming Your Authentic Self

Part of the healing activity of the Holy Fire® is to heal one's self which is a product of the cultural influences one develops into after being born. However, most people are aware to a greater or lesser extent of the possibility of becoming more than the person they were raised to be. These inklings of a more significant potential for our lives are coming from our Authentic Self and can be a pathway toward a more expansive way of living. The Culturally-Created Self mentioned previously is the personality that most people have, and it is essential to understand that religious trauma is part of the influence that shapes the Culturally-Created Self and contributes to spiritual amnesia in which one forgets that one is the Authentic Self. However, as an individual becomes aware of one's higher potential, one's philosophy of life changes and this starts a process in which one's personality begins to cast off aspects of the Culturally-Created Self in favor of qualities that arise from one's Authentic Self. This process is greatly accelerated when one becomes involved with Reiki and especially with Holy Fire® Reiki.

In Holy Fire® III, this process intensifies, and one's personality begins to heal more quickly making the possibility of assuming the qualities of one's Authentic Self more easily attainable. This healing process involves an awakening in which a transformation of the personality takes place so that one identifies more with the qualities of one's Authentic Self. Another way to describe this is to say that one's self-image merges with one's potential. Rather than thinking of one's potential as a possibility that feels different than who you are, you start to feel that your potential is no longer a potential, but more and more it is whom you are becoming. In other words, the process of becoming aware of your Authentic Self is a process of becoming your Authentic Self. One way to quicken this process is to think about your Authentic Self and feel what it must feel like to be the Authentic Self. Another method is to give yourself Holy Fire® Reiki daily while you repeat this affirmation: *I am my Authentic Self.*

The Spirit of the Earth

There is a spirit of the earth that is a divine being. This spirit watches over the earth and guides all the forces of nature. This spirit not only guides the material world but is part of it; it is present in all material things. The concept of Mother Nature is not just a metaphor but is a description of a spiritual presence that exists. This fact means that the earth and the material world are just as divine as any part of creation. Whenever you enjoy the beauty of a sunset, or sunbeams coming down through the clouds, or look at a mountain or a river or the ocean and have a feeling of peace and joy, you are experiencing the Spirit of the Earth. By giving Holy Fire® Reiki to anything in the material world, we can experience the divinity that exists in each tangible thing more clearly. As an example, once you have Holy Fire® Reiki energy, try sharing it with a cloud, a tree, a flower, the blue sky, a mountain or a river, or the ocean and each of these things will share its divinity with you and allow you to feel its peace and joy. You can also do this with other material things such as a table, a car, the curtains in a room, a painting or a lamp and discover divinity in these things too. One can often have astounding experiences by sharing Holy Fire® Reiki with the entire earth. By practicing this type of Reiki, you will connect with the Spirit of the Earth, and you'll know firsthand how enjoyable it is to be present in the material world. The concept of heaven on earth is something that is happening right now and has always been present. It is just a matter of having an open mind about this possibility and looking more deeply into the material world around you to be aware of this amazing reality.

Holy Fire® III Karuna Reiki® Symbols

The Holy Fire® III Karuna Reiki® symbols work the same basic way as the Usui Reiki symbols. They are keys that activate the different frequencies of healing energy available in Holy Fire® III Karuna Reiki®.

Several Ways To Activate Holy Fire® III Karuna Reiki® Symbols
1. Draw them on the palms of your hands, invoke their name 3 times, and pat them into your hands.
2. Visualize them in your mind's eye, and invoke their name 3 times.
3. Visualize them in the space between your thumb and first finger as you invoke their name 3 times.
4. Invoke their name 3 times, and pause to feel the energy activate.

These are just a few ways to activate the symbols. The important thing in activation is your intention. Because of this, you may be guided to activate them in ways other than what is mentioned here.

Preparing to Give a Holy Fire® III Karuna Reiki® Session
Before giving a Karuna Reiki® session it is important to prepare your energy field and the room before starting. To do this, draw the Holy Fire® symbol on your palms and clap them together 3 times saying "Holy Fire" each time. Then draw the Holy Fire® symbol on the front of your body. Hold the palm of one hand, in front of each of your chakras intending that the Holy Fire® energy is activated in each chakra beginning at the root chakra and moving up to the crown. Then draw Rama in front of your body, intending that it begin just beneath your feet and move up just beyond your crown. You could also visualize Rama on the soles of your feet. Then place Holy Fire® symbol on the walls, ceiling, and floor.

Working with the Holy Fire® III Karuna Reiki® Symbols During Sessions
In Holy Fire® Reiki sessions, the Holy Fire® symbol plays a prominent role. Some practitioners use this symbol exclusively while others use it in combination with the other symbols, activating the Holy Fire® symbol first.

Holy Fire® III Karuna Reiki® energy enhances one's intuition and because of this, guidance from the Holy Fire® plays an important role in giving Holy Fire® III Karuna Reiki® sessions. After preparing yourself for a session using the steps above, use the reiji ho method of intuitive guidance asking that the Holy Fire® guide you in knowing what kind of session is appropriate for your client at this time. Then follow your guidance.

Throughout the session rely on your intuition to know where to place your hands, and for how long, and which symbols to use. Sometimes the Holy Fire® energy will completely surround the client and treat the entire body and energy field at the same time. When this happens one will usually stay in that position a long time and may find that fewer hand positions are needed. In any case, always allow the Holy Fire® to guide you.

Another method is to use the Karuna I symbols with Holy Fire® in sequence - Zonar-Halu-Harth-Rama. Holy Fire®/Zonar is used to begin and prepares the client for deep healing. Holy Fire®/Halu heals deeply. Holy Fire®/Harth heals the heart, and fills any empty areas where negative energy has released, with loving energy. The session can be ended with Holy Fire®/Rama given to the feet to bring the client back into the body. Within this basic framework, intuition guides the session allowing you to use any of the Karuna I or II symbols as you are guided.

Karuna I Symbols

Zonar

Draw a Z, then draw the infinity symbol 3 times starting on the right.

Zonar is a good symbol to use at the beginning of a session as it prepares the client to receive deep healing. It also reduces or eliminates the pain associated with emotional healing by creating a kind of spiritual anesthetic effect.

Heals on Cellular Level
Sometimes we have experiences that are so powerful, and have lasted so long, that they actually become a part of our chemical makeup and are ingrained in our cells. Because of this, our cells can carry the memory of trauma, or even negative feelings and ideas that we brought with us from other lives. Zonar works on these hidden issues that have become imbedded in the cells of our bodies and helps to heal them. Zonar can be combined with the Usui distant symbol to send powerful healing energy.

Heals Past Life Issues
Zonar helps heal issues we have brought into this life from past lives. It also works interdimensionally with experiences we have had on other planets or in-between lives. To heal a past life issue, combine Zonar with the Usui distant symbol directing the energy to go into the past life and heal the cause.

Heals Child Abuse
Zonar works well to heal trauma resulting from child abuse and other issues that were so traumatic that the person has been unable to deal with them consciously, and has buried or stored the issues away from the conscious mind - often in the second chakra area. These are often things that are so overwhelming or unaccepted by our society that we are unable to talk with anyone about them. Zonar helps work on these deep issues, release and heal them. Sometimes they come to the conscious mind, and sometimes they are directly released without consciously knowing about them.

Heals Karmic Issues
Zonar can be invoked with the conscious intent to call upon Archangel Gabriel for assistance. This technique helps us with Karmic healing, and Archangel Gabriel can assist us in finding answers we need to help ourselves or others. To do this, think of the issue and connect with the energy and feelings around it. Then activate Zonar and send this energy up to Archangel Gabriel. Ask Gabriel

to take the karma of the issue and heal it for you. Ask also that if there is a lesson or understanding that is necessary for you to have in order for the healing to take place that it be made known to you. Be open and willing to follow any guidance that comes to you. The healing may continue after you stop sending healing energy, and ideas and memories may come welling up within your mind giving you the understanding you need.

Zonar prepares the client to receive the deep healing available from Halu.

Halu

Halu works in many ways like Zonar, but on a much deeper and more powerful level. Halu does not replace Zonar but complements it. Just as Reiki enhances all other healing modalities, Zonar complements Halu.

Draw a standard Zonar, then add the two lines into the center, and complete the pyramid on top.

Heals Unconscious Patterns

Use Halu to break up negative patterns in the unconscious mind which we use to insulate ourselves from the truth. This helps to shatter delusion and denial, while helping heal the shadow self. Halu helps us work through denial and blame of others for situations in our lives. Halu helps us accept that imperfect part of ourself so we can bring it into our conscious mind, love it, and heal it.

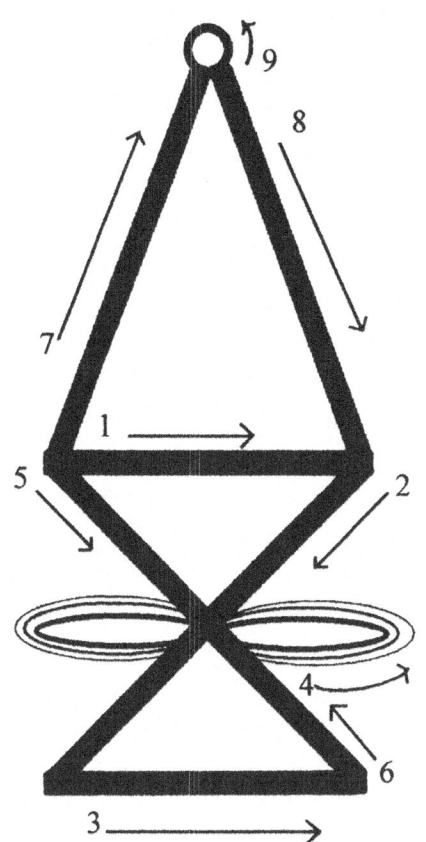

Heals the Shadow Self

The Shadow Self exists in the unconscious mind. It is composed of the parts of ourselves that we believe are unacceptable and so we try to hide them (denial) by shoving them down into the unconscious mind. We will often see these unwanted parts in others (projection) and dislike them for it. These unwanted parts often go into the second chakra. Halu can be directed to work on and heal the Shadow Self. This can be done by having the client focus on an unwanted experience or a behavior that has been difficult to heal. As they do this, ask them if any parts of their body feel tense or if there is an area within the body that they feel the cause of this problem is located. Sometimes this is in the second chakra. Activate Halu and direct it into the area.

Heals Sexual and Physical Abuse Issues

Trauma such as physical and sexual abuse is very painful. It is not always necessary to relive these experiences and re-experience the trauma in order to heal. The compassionate action of Halu (when used with Zonar) helps us release the energy from the abuse or pain without needing to re-experience the trauma. These issues can often be processed by simply having an understanding of what took place, without a need to feel all the emotions and pain. However, since the higher power is guiding the healing process, it will decide if feeling the pain is necessary to complete the healing and allow this to happen when it is appropriate for the client. When this happens, it usually takes place with only a small part of the pain coming into consciousness - just enough for the person to understand the feelings that are being healed.

Dispels Psychic and Psychological Attack

The only reason we are psychically attacked is because we are creating it. Halu can help us release the part of ourself that is creating the psychic attack, heal it and release it to the Higher Power. Often, as we come into our own power, we may not be confident because we have misused power in the past. This may cause us to be attacked by ourselves or by others who feel threatened by our increased power. Halu can be used to help us deal wisely and compassionately with our own power, and to release any part of ourselves that attracts psychic attack. Remember, the best way to deal with psychic attack is to accept that we have created this experience for ourselves from within ourselves as a way to know ourselves more completely and to heal. Focus on what you or the client is doing to create/attract the psychic attack and send Halu Reiki energy to it to heal/release it. Follow your inner guidance when doing this and allow yourself to learn as you heal. Halu will guide you to become a better healer.

Halu is a powerful healing tool

Halu can activate a laser-like beam of healing light, which can be focused on a less-than light area, and facilitate intense healing. It is helpful with physical healing of tumors and cysts and many other imbalances. When used with the aura clearing technique, it takes on the energy of a spiritual surgery tool which has the ability to break through even the densest concentrations of less than light energies. Halu goes to an area that contains less-than light energy and fills it with a very focused, concentrated beam of light which dissipates the denser energy.

After you have used Zonar and Halu to prepare the person for healing, and to do deep healing work, you will now be ready to fill the area with love by using Harth.

Harth

Draw the cross with the first line going down. Then draw the left and right sides and then the circles.

Harth heals the heart and all issues relating to the heart. It can also be used to fill in a healed area with love where negative energy or blocks have been removed.

Helps Heal Relationships

Harth can be used to heal relationships of all kinds. When two people are involved in a relationship, there is a third entity that exists - the relationship itself. If there is difficulty in the relationship, or if you simply want to improve your relationship, use Harth along with the Usui distant symbol to send Harth to the relationship. This will create a loving and compassionate feeling between the two people so they will more easily solve any problems that may have come up, and will enjoy each others company much more. Harth can improve a relationship that is already good! However, some relationships are co-dependent and not healthy for those involved. If this is the case, and it is time for the relationship to end, then Harth will help it end in a healthy way. Because Reiki is guided by the Higher Power, you will not be able to use Harth to get someone to enter into a romantic relationship with you against their will - it cannot be used to control people, only to empower them to come from love and to make wise decisions for themselves.

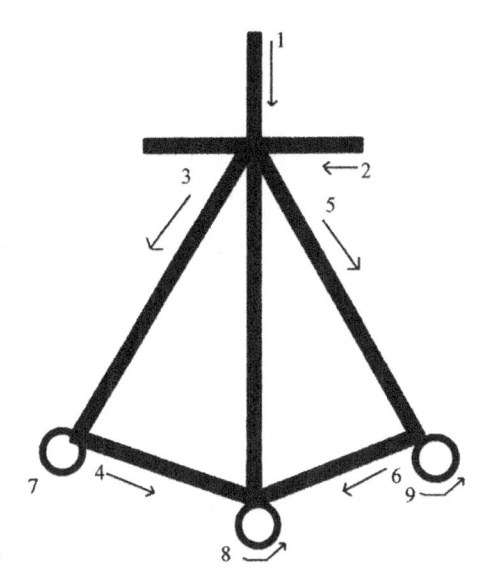

Develops Good Habits

If you want to develop a good habit, the best way to do this is to allow yourself to love what you want to do. When you look at all the habits that are healthy for a person to have, you will always be able to find some group or someone who loves that activity. There are people who love to cook and eat healthy food, or who love to exercise, or who love to meditate, or who love their work, or who love a balanced life. Sometimes we have trauma around things that are healthy for us. Harth can help us heal the trauma so we develop a natural love of things that are healthy for us to do. If there is a habit you would like to create for yourself, write it on a piece of paper, put it between your hands, and send Harth to it. Do this everyday, and also spend time doing the thing you want to develop a habit for. You will find it easier and easier to be involved with the new activity and soon you will love to do it. Try this, it works!

Heals Addictions

If a person is addicted to something, it usually means that they have a problem with their heart. A person will turn to drugs, alcohol, or destructive relationships and behaviors because there is something in their life that isn't fulfilling a need for love. Harth will restore the balance within their heart so that they love life. When a person loves life it is very unlikely that they are going to become addicted to something that

41

is harmful. If you love yourself, you will take good care of yourself. Use the Usui distant symbol to send Harth to the addiction.

Develops Compassionate Action
Compassionate action is the most essential part of the spiritual life. It is the key to both personal happiness and planetary healing. Harth can help develop the motivation for compassionate action by healing the heart. The wisdom that comes from the heart becomes available to guide us in all our actions. Harth helps us heal within ourselves so we can openly love others unconditionally. A wonderful revelation that comes to all who practice compassionate action is that it is not a sacrifice to do so, but a joy and a blessing.

Contact Spiritual Beings
Harth can be used to receive blessings from spiritual beings such as Jesus, Mother Mary, the Archangels, the Holy Spirit, and God, who are the embodiment of everything spiritual. Use the Usui distant symbol and send Harth to these spiritual beings. Ask for their blessing so your heart will be healed and you will be better able to help others. You will discover that love is the greatest power.

"The Original Reiki Ideals" state Reiki is "The secret art of inviting happiness" and Harth is a symbol that can do just that. Use Harth often to create love in your heart for yourself, others, or for anything in life worth doing, having or being.

After you have used Zonar, Halu and Harth, and are ready to complete the session, you can go on to Rama.

Rama

Rama is used for grounding. It is excellent to use at the end of a session.

Heals Lower Chakras
The use of Rama opens and heals the lower chakras helping a person be more fully present, alert, and focused. Often in healing work we encounter people who have a large portion of their energy outside their bodies. By using Rama on the client's feet, the feet chakras are opened and this will pull the person back into their body. This technique also pulls negative energy or blockages from anywhere in the person's energy system, out the feet and can often release pain. It is great for grounding.

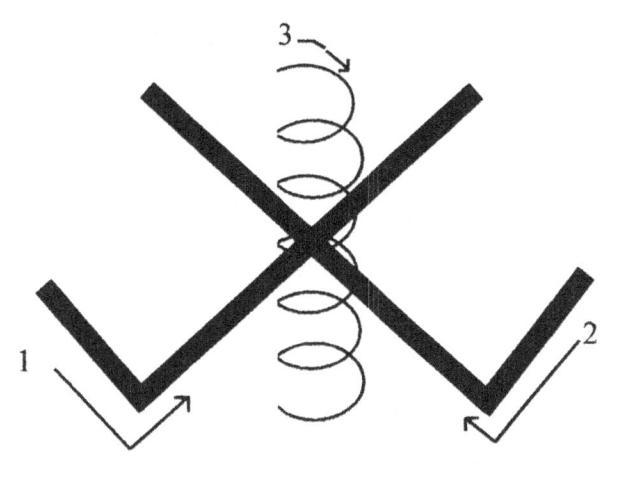

Clears the Mind
If you or your client are feeling out of sorts, confused, dizzy, or feel your mind is congested, use Rama on yourself to clear your mind. One way is to imagine Rama on the soles of your feet. This will open the feet chakras, allowing soothing earth energy to flow into your system. At the same time, all confusing energies that may have accumulated in your aura are channeled into the earth to be recycled. This is very refreshing and is great to use at the end of the work day or anytime you feel the need for a break!

Clears a Room of Negative Energies
You can prepare/clear your healing space or any other room by imagining Rama in the center of the room, the four corners of the ceiling, and floor. This will ground the room and allow any negative energies that may have accumulated to flow away at the same time positive energies from above fill the room. Another way you can do this is to draw Rama in the center of the room visualizing it filling the whole room. As you do this, focus your intent on clearing the space of any less-than light energies, and replacing them with the purest spiritual love. This is great to do at meetings or discussion groups where ideas are being exchanged as it brings clarity and decisiveness.

Harmonizes Upper Chakras with Lower Chakras
As Rama clears the lower chakras, it allows the higher consciousness of the upper chakras to manifest in the physical world. Rama also helps us release fear of success and fear of failure. It empowers us to actualize our spiritual purpose here on Earth, and to make use of Divine guidance in our everyday lives.

Creates Determination and Completion
This characteristic of Rama is what helps us to move beyond simply feeling compassion for something or someone, to being able to take determined action on that compassion. Rama helps us take the first step toward our goal, and assists us in remaining focused throughout the entire process so we can complete the things we start. Yes!

Manifests Material Goals
The process of manifestation involves being able to connect with universal creative consciousness through our spiritual body, then understand it as thoughts in the mental body, become excited about it in our emotional bodies, and take action on it with our physical bodies. Harmony between the upper and lower chakras is important if we are to have a meaningful effect on the world. Rama acts like a healing magnet, harmonizing the upper with the lower chakras, and pulling the creativity of higher consciousness through our whole system so that we can manifest it in our physical world. Archangel Michael's presence, and that of other enlightened beings, can often be felt when utilizing Rama to manifest goals that will help others.

Completing a Session
During a healing session, a person often leaves their body so that the guides can work more easily on the energy system to facilitate healing. Also, while out of the body, a person often receives new insights and guidance about their situation, but this does not always come into consciousness. Rama can be used at the end of a session to bring the client back into their body, grounding them to the earth, and allowing any insights received to come into consciousness so they can take action on them.

Karuna II Symbols

Gnosa

Circle is clockwise and drawn last

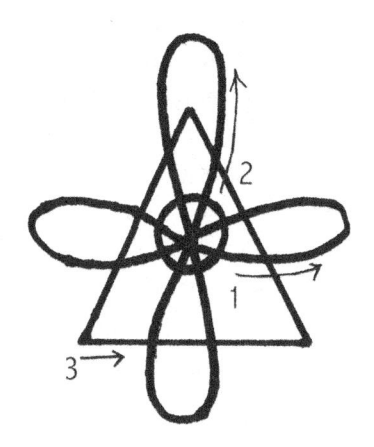

Gnosa heals the mind and links you more strongly with the Higher Self. Draw the propellers first, starting where the numbers are located, then the triangle, ending with the circle.

Connects the Higher Self with Lower Self

Gnosa brings the Higher Self into the physical body. Because of this, Gnosa can be used for very deep healing. It penetrates very deeply and lifts out emotional pain, often bringing an awareness of the true cause of the pain in a way that completes the healing.

Improves Learning Ability

Gnosa opens the mind allowing new ideas to more easily integrate into the mind. Because it works with the nervous system, it helps you learn physical things as well, such as dancing, martial arts, sports of all kinds, even playing musical instruments. It is great for studying and taking tests.

Heals Communication

By improving mental clarity, Gnosa helps us organize our minds and improve communication. It is useful for both speaking and writing. It can also be used for research projects, guiding you to the best sources of information and helping you comprehend their meaning.

Increases Creativity

Gnosa brings the higher mind into our everyday consciousness increasing clarity and inspiring us with new ideas. Gnosa adds depth to all our projects, and connects us with those enlightened beings who can guide us in their development and fulfillment. Gnosa works well with Rama allowing the Higher Self to manifest our creativity on the physical plane.

Iava (ee-ah-vah)

Draw the "3" first, then the swirl on it's back.

Claim Your Power
Sometimes there are others in our lives who try to control how we live. If we have a goal or a way of being that we want to create for ourselves, but there are those who don't want us to, it can make our achievements more difficult. Our plans and goals can become clouded by the negative intentions of others. This could be happening now, or there could be a residue of controlling thoughts and feelings in the subconscious mind left over from the past. This often happens because we have given up some of our power to those around us because of guilt and fear. Iava helps you break free from the expectations and projections of others and take back your power so you can create your life the way you want it to be.

Heals Codependence
Sometimes people make unconscious agreements with those whom they are close to that are not healthy and actually encourage each other to remain unhealed. These unconscious agreements prevent those involved from improving themselves. Iava helps you heal codependence allowing you to break free from an unhealthy sense of responsibility you may have with those whom you are close to.

Heals Reality Awareness
Iava helps us, and those around us, respect one another's independent realities. It helps us learn and understand what our reality should truly be based on who we really are inside rather than the expectations of others.

Empowers Your Goals
Iava helps us act on our plans even if others are not happy with our decisions. It helps us connect with the joyous outcome of our goals, which empowers us to achieve them.

Heals the Earth
Iava is truly an Earth healing energy, and can help us connect with the consciousness of trees, flowers, crystals, clouds, etc. Try Iava on your house plants. Iava works well with Harth to heal addictions.

Shanti

Draw the angle first, then the curved lines.

Shanti Brings Peace and Creates Trust in Life
Shanti can work with our connection to the flow of life allowing us to heal the past, create harmony in the present, and release the future. This process of letting go creates an effortlessness to our living process allowing us to enjoy life more deeply. People who have a tendency to worry, because things seem to have gone wrong in the past, often grow to expect things to go wrong in the future. Since Shanti helps heal the past, it brings peace into the now and helps free us from worry about the future.

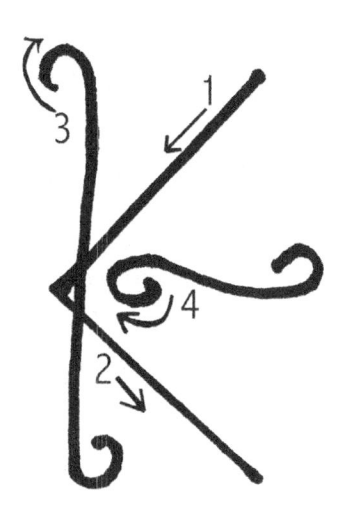

Heals Insomnia
Shanti releases fear and creates a gentle peaceful feeling. Because of this, it can help heal insomnia and help you get a good night's sleep. It is also good for healing nightmares.

Heals Fear and Panic
Shanti is also very helpful in treating panic attacks or chronic fatigue. This is because it helps calm fears and bring peace. Many people with these disorders worry about the future, they think about all the things that could go wrong, rather than focusing on their goals. This is very draining, and they become weak and very tired. Shanti creates such a soothing state of being they are able to focus more on the now, and do so in a peaceful way.

Manifests the Best Results
When combined with Rama or Kriya, Shanti can bring harmony to the realization of one's goals making them seem effortless to achieve.

Increases Clairvoyance
Meditate with the point of Shanti going into the third eye. Maintain this single-pointed focus and it will clear the brow chakra enhancing clairvoyance.

Kriya

This double Choku Rei is used for physical manifestation and for healing the human race.

Grounding
To use Kriya for grounding, visualize each side of the symbol going down each leg. Place the upper part in your hips with the spirals in your feet. This will create a strong connection to the earth and bring your consciousness more fully into your body. This will also help guide your path through life in a very practical way.

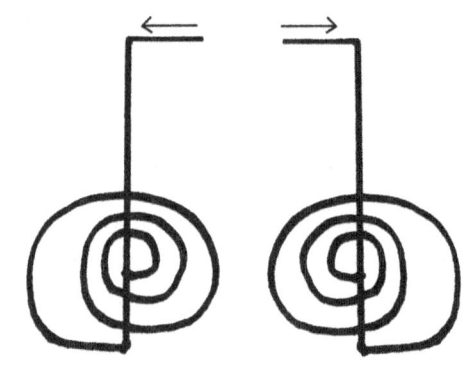

Manifests Goals
Kriya can be used to manifest goals. One way to work with Kriya to manifest goals is to write your goal on a piece of paper in the form of an affirmation. For example, if you would like to have a Reiki practice where you see 20 people a week, you would create an affirmation like; "I have 20 Reiki clients every week." Then draw Kriya on the paper and hold it between your hands and do Kriya Reiki on it everyday. At the same time, you must be working to create your goal, by creating a plan and acting on it. If your goal is for your highest good, you will find valuable "coincidences" occurring that help you manifest your goal. Kriya Reiki will reach out to all the people and resources needed to help you create your goal and make it a joy to manifest.

Creates Priorities
Kriya is helpful if you feel stuck with many thoughts, and have difficulty focusing on what you need to do. It will help you sort out your priorities, and focus on the things that are important to manifest in your life now. It also helps you focus your energy on them.

Heals the Human Race
Kriya can be used to heal all the people of Earth, helping them work together in harmony.

Holy Fire® Symbol

This is the master symbol for Holy Fire® III Karuna Reiki®. It is drawn by starting at the bottom and going in the direction of the arrow up the left side, then completing each of the 3 flames, and coming back down to the bottom. This symbol represents the Holy Fire® which is a spiritual flame. The above drawing is an outline, but the actual image is a living flame that is composed of beautiful colors which are constantly changing with the center of the flame being exceedingly bright. After you've been initiated it's possible that when you draw the symbol to activate it for use in your Reiki sessions, you will actually see this beautiful flame in your mind's eye, and when giving Holy Fire® Reiki in sessions, you may see flames around or coming from your hands.

To use the Holy Fire® in Reiki sessions activate it by simply intending to use it. This can be done by drawing the image on your hands, or in the air in front of you, or over or on the part of the client's body you'd like to treat. You can also say the words Holy Fire® to yourself, or connect with the energy by looking at the flame in your body. The Holy Fire® energy often flows throughout the client's body and aura and can sometimes appear as a flame surrounding the body. It works in several ways: It can burn up byoki which is negative ki, release malefic spirits or other entities which are not compatible with the client's path of development, and it can purify - these processes are the first step of healing. The Holy Fire® can further promote healing by helping the parts of the physical body that have been weakened or damaged to be restored, and can also restore the emotions, the mind and the spirit, and also work on the core of one's being. It can also empower by imbuing your being with unusual vitality and confidence, and feelings of safety and peace. An important aspect of Holy Fire® healing is a wonderful feeling of being loved. Use the Holy Fire® symbol before using any of the Karuna I or II symbols as the Holy Fire® will empower each of the symbols.

Notes

Holy Fire® Meditation

Holy Fire® meditation works best if done every day and if done in the morning. Twice a day is better..However, you can also do it whenever you have the time. This is a very powerful meditation that has the ability to increase your connection to Holy Fire® thus making it more powerful and effective. It can uplift your consciousness, heal you in profound ways, and bring wonderful blessings including physical relaxation, mental clarity including improved ability to visualize, enhanced healing skills, and the expansion of consciousness. It can also bring Divine Revelation - the highest form of inner knowing in which the Source communicates with you directly.

This meditation method also has the amazing tendency to surround your body, and energy field, and every aspect of your life with a soft cloud of Holy Fire® consciousness. Its value increases with regular use.

1. Sit quietly in a comfortable position with your hands on your legs or other part of your body, breathing slowly and deeply with your eyes closed.

2. Draw the Holy Fire® symbol in front of you or simply become aware of it in your abdomen or above your head or wherever you may discover it to be. You may see a simple outline of the flame, or it can be or eventually become a vibrant living multicolored flame of great beauty.

3. Hold the image of the Holy Fire® in your mind in front of you and repeat Holy Fire® three times. Say it out loud if no one will hear you or to yourself if others are around. Hold the visual image of the symbol steadily in your mind for several minutes and up to 20 minutes. You may use a clock or watch and briefly open your eyes to check the time when you sense it is up, or use a gentle alarm clock such as a meditation app or the Zen Alarm Clock app which you can download to your cell phone.

4. If thoughts arise in your mind, as soon as you notice them, brush them away and come back to the image of the flame. Do not worry if you catch your mind wandering away from the image, or if you start thinking about other things. If you discover this has happened, do not berate yourself. Simply direct your mind back to the image. As you continue this practice each day, your ability to hold the image steadily will strengthen. And in fact, the flame can become so fascinating that it will be difficult not to look at it. If you have trouble visualizing, do the best you can. If you cannot visualize at all, and repeated attempts have not brought improvement, draw the symbol on a piece of paper or use the image in this manual; focus on it in the same way with your eyes open and relaxed. After a while, experiment with closing your eyes and retaining the image.

5. Allow yourself to merge with the flame. The flame may also begin to guide you. As this happens, follow the flame. It will guide you into wonderful experiences.

6. When you are finished meditating, take a couple of deep breaths, bring your awareness to your eyes. Then slowly open your eyes and return.

Soul and Spirit Defined

Soul and spirit are words commonly used in metaphysical work. However, each speaker, group or school will usually have its own understanding that they intend to convey in their use. The following is how these words are used in Holy Fire® Reiki.

Soul is that part of us that is the repository of all our experiences from this life, from all past lives, and in-between lives. It also contains all the attitudes, values and beliefs we've formed about our experiences as well as the decisions we've made about ourselves and about life, and what we've learned. It contains many parts, some conscious, but many subconscious. It is also the home of the ego. There are usually many levels of awareness within each soul and each soul is different depending on the experiences each has had and the way the soul interpreted those experiences. There can be parts that have been traumatized and not recovered, parts that are sick, angry and sad, injured, and have low levels of consciousness. There can also be evolved parts that have healthy positive qualities such as wisdom, kindness, love, joy, vitality, and have highly evolved levels of consciousness. The soul is who we are as a unique individual. And it is at the soul level that Reiki attunements and Placements are received.

The spirit is that part of us that is connected to Source, connected to God. The spirit can evolve too. This means that it can develop a greater connection to God. Since God is infinite, there is no limit to the development the spirit can experience. There will always be a higher level, a greater experience that will give access to more of God's resources, experiences and states of consciousness. Because the spirit connects to God, it is the spirit that provides mystical experiences including a feeling of oneness, of being connected with all other beings, all of life. It is through the spirit that we have a feeling of love toward everyone and everything. The spirit makes its awareness and resources available to the soul. As our spirit evolves and becomes more refined, so do our various levels and types of consciousness. And it is the spirit that experiences the Holy Fire® Ignitions and then sends the energy into the soul.

Growing in the Experience

It is possible to go beyond the Holy Fire® energy and experience something more profound. In many ways, this experience goes beyond meditation. When working on higher levels of consciousness, the less you do and the less the ego is involved, the higher you go. Because of this, there is very little for the student to do, yet what takes place can be more meaningful. Simply sit in a comfortable position. Have no agenda; let the Source, God decide what is next. Direct your attention inward and express gratitude that you are growing in the experience. Then simply wait.

Healing Spirit Attachments

The Holy Fire® Reiki Spirit Release technique is a powerful and compassionate Reiki technique. It releases spirits of all types into the authority of love and forgiveness. Love is the most powerful healing force in existence. In this technique, God's love expresses as the light. The light shines on the spirit and bathes it in God's love. Immersed in the power of love and the grace of forgiveness, the spirit releases willingly from the client into the light where it is healed by God.

There are many kinds of spirit attachments. Not all spirit attachments have malicious intent. Many consist of confused spirits who did not cross over into the light and may not know where they are or that they have attached to you. We call these discarnate spirits, and the Holy Fire® Spirit Release technique can help them cross into the light and go home to their loved ones. Some spirits even believe they are helping the person they attach to when they are not. In other situations, a spirit may come to help a child or a person in crisis and remain present after they are no longer needed.

Regardless of a spirit's intent, spirit attachments will almost always cause problems. They can cause physical weakness and illness, mental, emotional and spiritual dysfunction, problems with relationships, weaken one's creative abilities, cause disorientation and make debilitating conditions one might have worse. Because of this, the Holy Fire® Spirit Release technique is a valuable tool for Reiki practitioners. The method is compassionate to both the client and the spirit.

Holy Fire® Reiki energy carries with it the power and grace of divine forgiveness. This forgiveness does not come from our own energy but is given to us as a gift. Because its source is not our energy, the spirit cannot use it to try to maintain a connection with us. Coming from the third heaven or higher, it is more powerful than any energy to which the attaching spirit has access. Because of this, the process can easily release any attached spirit or spirit trying to cause problems.

It is important to understand that forgiveness is not granted because a spirit's behavior is accepted or approved. It means that by forgiving, you are not judging the spirit, nor wishing it harm. By forgiving the spirit, you go to a higher level of consciousness which prevents the spirit from having a way to attach to you. In this technique, the grace of forgiveness and the power of love flow into and around the attached spirit(s). As it does this, it dissolves all cords and connectors and sources of power and all effects from the spirit in this life and all past lives and releases the spirit into God's care so that God's plan for it manifests completely.

Because God's love is receiving the spirit, the spirit is more willing to leave the body gently with no resistance. There is virtually no "battle" as often seen in other spirit release or exorcism techniques.

It is important to simply let the spirit go with no interest in who it was, why it attached or what will happen to the spirit after release. The Reiki practitioner simply focuses attention on God's love. If your clients want to know more about the spirit, tell them that God's love is now revealed in the place where the spirit was attached and that they need to focus their attention on the God's love.

In order to use this process, a person must have taken either the Usui/Holy Fire® ART/Master Training or the Holy Fire® Karuna Reiki® Training, and have the use of the Holy Fire® symbol and energy. An alternate method of spirit release is available for those without Holy Fire® Reiki at http://www.reiki.org/reikinews/improvepractice.html

Part One: Releasing the Spirit
1. Place the Holy Fire® symbol on each palm chakra, then place your hands on your legs and give yourself Holy Fire® Reiki. Watch as it flows within you and around you.

2. Pray that your entire ego and all your personal energy be set to the side so that only the pure energy of the Holy Fire® and the power of God's love and forgiveness be involved in the spirit release process.

3. After sending Reiki for about five minutes, draw the Distant symbol and say this prayer: I pray that Holy Fire® Reiki along with God's love and forgiveness flow through all spirit(s) not part of God's plan, on every level of existence and flow through all their effects, all their cords and connectors and sources of power and through all their assignments and all those who have given them assignments.

4. Then say this prayer: I pray that Holy Fire® Reiki along with God's love and forgiveness completely release and heal all spirit(s) not part of God's plan. I also ask that all the effects of the spirit(s), release and heal, along with all cords and connectors, and sources of power, and all its assignments, and all those who have given it assignments also be completely released and healed. I ask that God's will for these spirits and all their effects be completely manifest.

5. Continue to give Holy Fire® Reiki for a few more minutes to allow this to take place.

6. Then say this prayer: I am grateful to God that this healing has taken place.

Part Two: Healing the Part That Allowed the Spirit to Attach
It is necessary to heal the weakness in the part of the client to prevent other spirits from using the same part to form an unhealthy connection to the client. Follow these instructions to heal this part.

1. After the Holy Fire® has released the spirit(s), use the Distant symbol to send Holy Fire® Reiki to the part(s) of the person that allowed the spirit(s) to attach. Send Holy Fire® Reiki for about five minutes.

2. As you do so, say this prayer: I pray that God's love and healing flow through the part of the person that allowed the spirit to be present so that it is completely healed and cannot be used by unhealthy spirits ever again. Please take this part to the third heaven or higher where it will dwell in God's love and peace forever.

3. Then say: I pray to God that this process will continue for as long as is necessary until it is complete according to God's love and wisdom.

4. Continue to send Reiki while you express your gratitude that this healing process has taken place.

5. Ask the client to return and talk about the experience.

Notes

Experiences, Placements and Ignitions Explained

Experiences

These include the Ocean of Holy Love, Holy Love Experience I, II and III, Heavenly Banquet Hall Experience, Holy Fire® Healing Experience and Healing in the River of Life Experience. The time to allocate for an Experience is between 30-45 minutes depending on group size and the time spent sharing after the Experience. Experiences provide healing, insight and guidance on one's situation in life.

We can use Experiences in a variety of situations.

Given in a Reiki Session

1. Experiences can be provided by themselves instead of a hands-on session. When doing this, you could explain at the end of a hands-on session how the Experience works and that it could be done in the next scheduled session instead of a regular hands-on session or you could explain how the Experience works and suggest it for the current session.

2. You can also do Experiences with a hands-on session. This option can create a more powerful session. First, explain how the Experience works and that you will stop talking after giving a few of the hand positions, and the client will continue internally with the Experience as you continue to give the remaining hand positions. Finish the session giving Reiki to the feet, then when you are done with the hands-on segment, say these words: *When you feel ready, take a couple of deep breaths, bring your awareness to your eyes, and slowly open your eyes and return.* Have a glass of water ready to offer to the client, ask them to describe what they experienced and write a brief description on their Client Information Form. Please note that when using the Holy Fire® Healing Experience with a hands-on session, when you get to the part of the Experience where the beam of light is shining on location of the shape, I suggest that you place your hands over this area. Treat and then go back to complete the regular hand placement sequence after you have come to the end of the verbal part of the Experience.

Given as Part of a Reiki Talk

You can also give Experiences as part of a Reiki talk. Page 92 provides an outline for this use.

Given in Reiki Classes

Experiences are given in Reiki classes to facilitate healing and to prepare the student for the Placements and Ignitions that take place in class. The Healing in the River of Life Experience is given In the Master classes, and in this context, this Experience provides the student with the ability to conduct Placements as part of Reiki classes. When the Healing in the River of Life Experience is given outside a Reiki class, such as when part of a Reiki talk or during a Reiki session, it does not provide the participant the ability to give Placements but facilitates healing and personal guidance only.

Placements
Placements are used only in Reiki classes for Reiki I, II or I and II and the first part of Reiki Master where instruction and practice time are included. Placements provide the same benefit as the attunement and give students the ability to use Reiki in Reiki I and empower the symbol(s) in Reiki II and the first part of Reiki Master. Class time of between 6-12 hours is recommended for each level depending on class size and teacher preference.

Ignitions
Ignitions are given in the Master Teacher classes including the Usui/Holy Fire® III Reiki Master Training and the Holy Fire® III Karuna Reiki® Master Training. Ignitions are similar to attunements and give the student the ability to use the Master symbols in Reiki sessions and to conduct the Placements and Ignitions in Reiki classes.

Unique Format for Experiences, Placements and Ignitions

In the Usui/Holy Fire® Reiki classes, there are no guided meditations or attunements conducted by the teacher. The Holy Fire® energy conducts these procedures directly, therefore, during the Placements, Experiences and Ignitions, there is no physical interaction between the teacher and the student. The teacher doesn't go behind the student, or in front, and doesn't touch the student, or draw symbols, and so forth. The teacher simply sits in a chair and facilitates a short experience to place the student into a receptive state and then lets the Holy Fire® take over. This is a remarkable effect and a demonstration of the power and higher consciousness of the Holy Fire® energy. And in fact, the less the teacher is involved, the more powerful and effective the experience becomes. This feature of Holy Fire® Reiki can be especially meaningful as each experience is individually guided by the Holy Fire® to address the specific needs of each student. We call the guided meditations experiences because the teacher doesn't actually guide them. The attunements are called Placements and Ignitions because the Holy Fire® guides the experience directly, and ignites the Holy Fire® as a living flame within each student.

Before teaching Usui/Holy Fire® classes for the first time, the teacher may be unsure if the Placements, Experiences, and Ignitions will work. Do not worry. This is a feeling many new teachers have had. Because you have taken the Holy Fire® Master training and had the Holy Fire® energy installed in your field, you are ready, and any concern you might have will not affect the experiences your students have. Simply trust that they will work and follow the procedure, and they will work amazingly well.

Ocean of Holy Love Experience

The Ocean of Holy Love is an ocean of liquid light that contains many colors and frequencies which provide healing for a wide range of conditions and issues. The energy is very soothing and feels wonderful. The student can dive under the water and breathe in the liquid light. When doing this the liquid light flows through the student's entire body, relaxing and healing. There may also be flames of Holy Fire® both above and below the surface. The flames do not burn; they feel wonderful as they purify, heal, guide, empower, and protect. This experience can be conducted in class or a Reiki share group or at a Reiki talk or as a stand-alone Reiki session.

The experiences a student can have may include swimming and floating on the surface, diving and swimming under the surface, breathing in the light, and having waves of the ocean wash over one's body. Many other experiences can take place as well as each experience is uniquely guided by the Holy Fire® to provide what the student needs. Some will have visual experiences, others will feel the energy flowing around and within, and for some the experience will take place mostly in the unconscious parts of the mind while the student remains in a state of calm and peace.

The experience is directed by the Holy Fire® so it's important not to try to direct it yourself, but to let go completely and trust; simply allow yourself to be guided and to go with the flow.

Script
Students can be seated or lying on the floor or can change positions during the experience, moving to the floor or returning to their chair

1. "This is the Ocean of Holy Love Experience."

2. "Close your eyes and take a couple of deep breaths."

3. "It's a beautiful day, warm and sunny. You're walking down a path in a beautiful forest. As you breathe into yourself, you breathe in the life energy of the forest and with each step that you take, feel the energy of the earth flowing up through the bottoms of your feet."

4. "As you walk along, you notice up ahead it is getting lighter, and that you are coming to the edge of the forest."

5. "As you walk out of the forest, you notice the path is getting sandy and you hear the sound of the ocean."

6. "Walking out onto the beach, the ocean is before you."

7. "It's a wonderful day, and slowly you begin to walk along the beach."

8. "As you walk along, you notice a log has been washed up on the beach, creating a nice place to sit and lean up against. Go ahead and sit and relax against the log"

9. "This is no ordinary ocean, it is the Ocean of Holy Love."

10. "Listen to the sound of your breathing and imagine it is the sound of the waves washing up onto the beach and then flowing back in the ocean."

11. "The Ocean of Holy Love is guiding you. Follow the guidance."

Stop Talking. Wait 15-26 minutes. During this time, say this prayer: "I surrender this entire Experience to God, Jesus, Holy Spirit, and the Holy Fire®." Then simply relax enjoying the energy you are receiving.

After 15-26 minutes say, "You can continue with your experience as long as you feel guided to do so." (Pause) "And when you are ready, take a couple of deep breaths, bring your awareness to your eyes, and slowly open your eyes and come back."

Ask the students to write their experiences in their notebooks. When they are done, ask if they would like to share their experience with the class

Holy Love Experience

The Holy Love Experience may be included in each of the Holy Fire® classes as the teacher feels guided. Holy Love Level One is given on day two or three toward the beginning of the classes including level II, ART/ Master, and Karuna. Holy Love Level Two and Three can take place in the Master classes. Level Two could be included on the second or third day and level Three is done on the third day, but only if you have time. Holy Love (any level) can also be used at a Reiki Share group or included in a talk about Holy Fire® Reiki to give people an experience of Holy Fire®, or it could be conducted by itself as a Reiki session.

Holy Love I Experience
Divine Love is installed more clearly and deeply into one's soul. Divine love is a special kind of love that is more highly refined and has a higher level of consciousness than human love. It is simultaneously many things: It is a feeling of being loved by a kind and wonderful energy. It is a feeling of being cared for by an energy that knows you intimately and is fully capable of taking care of all your needs. It is a feeling of being safe. It is a healing and enhancement of your own ability to love so that there are no unhealthy feelings associated with it. It is a love that you have for yourself and others that feels very natural and normal. It is an energy similar to life energy that flows throughout your body and your entire being, and is part of who you are. It can be present in your space without having to have someone or something as its focus. It soothes, relaxes, nurtures and heals very deeply.

Script
Students can be sitting in a circle holding hands or not holding hands or some can lay on the floor or on a couch or be seated in a chair as each chooses. Meditation music can be played in the background.

1. "Imagine it is a beautiful sunny day. Imagine you are walking through a beautiful forest."

2. "As you breathe into yourself, imagine you are breathing in the life essence of the forest. And with each step you take, imagine the energies of the earth are flowing up through the bottoms of your feet."

3. "As you walk along allow yourself to experience the trees, plants, flowers and grass, and to merge with the life and the harmony and peace of the forest."

4. "As you continue to walk along you notice that up ahead it is getting lighter and you realize you are coming to the edge of the forest."

5. "As you leave the forest, before you is a beautiful river. It is the River of Life. There are beautiful flowers growing along the river bank and there is a path following alongside the river. Follow the path alongside the river."

6. "Eventually you come to a bend in the river. There is a light breeze blowing causing the surface of the river to have small ripples."

7. "The sun is shining off the rippled surface of the water creating a glittering, shimmering light. You realize this is no ordinary light, but is a spiritual light coming from the highest heaven."

8. "You allow the light to enter your soul."

9. "Allow the light to guide you."

Then stop talking and allow the light to guide each student. Wait 15-26 minutes or so. During this time, say this prayer: "I surrender this entire Experience to God, Jesus, Holy Spirit, and the Holy Fire®." Then simply relax and enjoy the energy you are receiving.

Keep track of the time using a clock or your cell phone set to airport mode, or otherwise when you sense it is time for the students to come back say words to this effect: "Whenever you are guided to do so and at the pace that feels right for you, take a few breaths, bring your awareness to your eyes and slowly open your eyes and come back."

After it appears that most are back, ask them to take time to write down their experiences and to integrate.

Wait until all are done writing, then ask "Who would like to share his or her experience?"

Holy Love II Experience
In this Experience, Holy Love scans the person's timeline in this life to find the most important experience that needs healing to improve the person's health and wellbeing. This could be a physical injury, or it could also be an emotional or psychological trauma. It then works with the aspects of the personality and the energies involved to heal the issue.

Procedure
To conduct the Holy Love II experience, explain the purpose of Holy Love II as described above. Then follow the same instructions for Holy Love I. A variation could be that they go up into the mountains by a waterfall and see the glittering, shimmering light reflecting off the pool of water at the waterfall.

Holy Love III Experience
In this experience, Holy Love takes the person back to the time of conception, gestation, birth and post-birth. The purpose of this experience is to heal everything needing healing from the time of conception to post-birth. This can include things that were going on between and with the parents, ancestral issues, experiences in the womb, and birth trauma. Sometimes the student is aware of what has happened, and sometime they may not know what specifically has healed but that it was something meaningful.

Procedure
To conduct the Holy Love III Experience, explain the purpose of Holy Love III as described above. Then follow the same instructions for Holy Love I. A variation could be a mountain spring in which the sun is reflected off the surface of the rippling pool of water created by the spring.

Holy Love IV Experience
This Experience can be used for participants with no Reiki training, at Reiki Share Groups, and with those who have Usui/Tibetian or Usui/Holy Fire® I, II, III or higher and those with any level of Karuna Reiki® training or with those who have Reiki training from any school or lineage and will also work with a combination of participants from any of these groups.

The consciousness within the Holy Fire® energy will evaluate where each person is at and provide the type of energy and experience that is appropriate to heal or to take each to the next level of their development as a student on the spiritual path and/or as a healer.

The energy will work deeply within the subconscious mind of each participant. Because of this, some participants may simply feel calm and relaxed. And others may see colors or feel the energy flowing through them or have other inner experiences. However, it is important to know that the most important effects take place below the students' level of awareness and then rise slowly to the level of the students' conscious mind. Because of this, each may not be aware of the full effect of what has happened until hours or days after the experience is over.

Procedure
To conduct the Holy Love IV Experience, explain the purpose of Holy Love IV as described above. Then follow the same instructions as for Holy Love I. A variation could be a mountain spring in which the sun is reflecting off the surface of the rippling pool of water created by the spring.

Heavenly Banquet Hall Experience

The Heavenly Banquet Hall exists in the third heaven and is a place of spiritual nourishment. This experience can be added if you have time. It can also be given at a Reiki Share group or a Reiki talk.

Students can be sitting, lying on the floor, and can change positions during the experience if they want to.

1. "The Heavenly Banquet Hall exists high in the heavens. It is a place of spiritual nourishment."

2. "We are now rising up to the Heavenly Banquet Hall high in the Heavens."

3. "We are now sitting around a large, round banquet table."

4. "As you look up there are beautiful stained glass windows, and through one of the windows you notice a very special kind of light that is shining through and into your eyes, and it enters your soul. The light is guiding you. Follow the light and allow it to guide you."

Then stop talking and allow the light to guide each student. Wait 15-26 minutes or so. During this time say prayers giving thanks for the experiences the Holy Fire® is providing each student. And also spend time going inward and being in your own experience.

Keep track of the time using a clock or your cell phone set to airport mode. When you sense it is time for the students to come back say words to this effect: "Whenever you are guided to do so and at the pace that is right for you, take a few breaths, bring your awareness to your eyes and slowly open your eyes and come back."

After it appears that most are back, ask them to take time to write down their experiences and to integrate.

Wait until all are done writing and ask, "Who would like to share his or her experience?"

Holy Fire® Healing Experience Explained

A Holy Fire® Healing Experience can be done which will provide a deeply healing experience. This Experience brings in high frequency healing energies that are more powerful and effective than those given during a regular Reiki session. If done before a regular Reiki session, it will make the session more effective by opening the aura and creating a more receptive state. It can be done on more than one client at a time. It must be done in private with no one watching, and with the client's eyes closed. This technique can be done with an individual during a Reiki session, at the end of a talk on Holy Fire® Reiki, or during a Holy Fire® Reiki class.

The most powerful results are achieved by doing a Holy Fire® Healing Experience first, followed by a standard Reiki session using all the hand positions.

Removing Negative Energy
The Holy Fire® Healing Experience is highly effective in removing negative energies from the client. It will remove negative energy in the physical body, aura and chakras, and work to help release any blocks the client chooses.

Before beginning the healing Experience, explain to the client that she must be willing to let go of the block and any other conditions in her life that the block may have created. She must be willing to make important changes in attitude about herself and her life concerning the issues involved, and to become aware of those issues in new ways. Have the client focus on the block with the intention of releasing it during the healing experience.

Empowering Goals
The Holy Fire® Healing Experience can also be used to empower goals. If there is a goal the client has had trouble achieving, it is likely that there is something that needs to heal before she can achieve it. There may be unconscious, negative feelings and thoughts about the goal that are blocking its achievement, such as fear of failure or fear of success. Having the client focus on these blocks will cause them to be released during the Holy Fire® Healing Experience.

During the Holy Fire® Healing Experience, it is also possible to receive insight about the goal and guidance for making plans. Sometimes a particular goal is not in harmony with a person's life path. If this is the case, the client may become aware of this during the Holy Fire® Healing Experience. Note that the block which is the cause of the issue is discovered during the preparation part of this process.

Have the client focus on the goal and be willing to take responsibility for doing whatever is necessary to achieve it while being open to new ideas and attitudes about it. A willingness to release unconscious, negative attitudes about the goal is also necessary.

Preparations for a Holy Fire® Healing Experience

Steps

The first step is to give the cause of the problem an identity. This will allow the client and practitioner to focus directly on the cause and release it. Giving the problem an identity can be very healing in itself as it allows one to bring the cause into awareness, where it can be dealt with. This involves finding the location of the block, and becoming aware of what it looks like.

Ask the client to open her workbook to a blank page and be ready to take notes. Let the client know you will be asking a series of simple questions and that there is no wrong answer and that whatever she or he comes up with will work. Ask her or him to accept the first answer that comes to mind.

1. Ask the client to think about the issue she would like to have healed. Note that it is not necessary for her to tell you what the issue is, just for her to think about it. This confidentiality can be very helpful for many clients as some issues are so sensitive that the client may not want to let anyone know what the issue is.

2. Ask her to close her eyes and meditate on the issue. Ask the client: "If the original cause of this issue were to be located somewhere in your physical body, where would it be?" This is often easy because the client will feel tension or pain in an area of the body when she thinks of the issue. If she has difficulty choosing an area, just ask the client to guess and assure her that there is no wrong answer. Whichever area she chooses will work.

3. Ask her to imagine that she is looking into the area she has chosen and ask her, "If this issue had a shape, what shape would it have?" Have the student write down a description of the shape in her notebook.

4. Do the same thing to find the color, texture, weight, temperature and sound that the shape makes so that the client has a clear energetic image of the block. Remember that any answer is okay and that the client doesn't have to answer all of the questions.

Holy Fire® Healing Experience

The Holy Fire® Healing Experience is similar to the Healing Attunement that we used to do except that it is done as a Holy Fire® Experience. The ability to facilitate this Experience in class and in your Reiki sessions is empowered within you during the River of Life Experience at the same time that it also gives the ability to use Placements instead of attunements. This experience is for healing a specific issue the client or student would like to heal and it can also be used to empower a goal as explained above. It can be done in class or in individual Reiki sessions.

After you've helped the client to find the location, shape, color, and so forth listed in the steps above, explain to the client how the Holy Fire® Healing Experience will work; that you'll help them get into a receptive state of mind by using a short guided meditation, and then will stop talking to allow the Holy Fire® energy to guide the process and provide the healing experience. Before you start the guided portion, begin playing soothing music such as Julie True, Music to Journal By, Vol. 1 or other similar music.

Then follow this script:

1. "This is the Holy Fire® Healing Experience. You can be sitting or lying on the floor or move during the experience if you feel you need to. Make yourself comfortable and take a few deep breaths."

2. "It's a beautiful day, warm and sunny. You're walking down a path in a beautiful forest. As you breathe into yourself, you breathe in the life energy of the forest and with each step that you take, feel the energy of the earth flowing up through the bottoms of your feet."

3. "As you walk along you notice another path going off to the right. You feel compelled to follow this path."

4. "As you follow this path, you come to a clearing in the forest and in the middle of the clearing is a small hill covered with soft grass."

5. "Climb up the hill, feel the grass rubbing against your legs."

6. "When you get to the top of the hill, lie down in the soft grass. Feel the grass and the earth beneath your body and gaze up into the sky."

7. "Gaze up into the sky and see the beautiful white clouds. As you are gazing up at the clouds, a beautiful beam of light begins to shine down through the clouds."

8. "This is no ordinary light: it comes from high in the Heavens. The light shines all around you and flows into you, filling you with warmth and feelings of safety and love."

9. "The light focuses directly on the shape. Focus on the shape and be willing to let it go."

10. "Now gaze directly into the light and as you do so, the light begins to guide you."

11. "Follow the light."

Stop talking and wait 20 minutes. During this time, say this prayer: "I surrender this entire Experience to God, Jesus, Holy Spirit, and the Holy Fire®." Then simply relax and enjoy the energy you are receiving.

After 20 minutes or so, say, "You can continue with your experience as long as you feel guided to do so." Then after waiting a short time, say, "When you are ready, take a couple of deep breaths, bring your awareness to your eyes and slowly open your eyes and return. Then after a short time say, "What does your shape look like now?" Then after another short time say, "Take some time to write down your experiences in your notebooks and include any changes to the shape."

After all have stopped writing ask students/client to share about their experiences.

Empowered by the River of Life Experience

This Experience is used in the Usui/Holy Fire® Online Master Class and the Holy Fire® Online Karuna Reiki® Master class. It gives students the ability to give Online Placements when they teach, use the *Holy Fire® Online Healing Experience*, and facilitate the online *Empowered by the River of Life Experience* in their Master classes. This Experience will also allow all those students who teach other styles of Reiki in person, to continue to do so. This ability is possible because this Experience will empower the student with the Holy Fire® in such a way to work in harmony with the other systems of Reiki a student may hold.

Students can be seated or lying on the floor and can change positions if they choose to. They start their music, such as Julie True's, *Music to Journal By, Volume 1*, or any soothing or meditative music. Ask the students to relax.

Use This Script to Explain the River of Life
"There is a sacred mountain range where the peaks of the mountains reach up energetically into the higher heavens. The rain and snow that fall on these mountains come from the highest spiritual heaven. This water flows down the mountains and over beautiful waterfalls then flows together to form a sacred river. The river also flows through a volcanic area where it is warmed to jacuzzi temperature. The water in the River of Life is crystal clear and completely pure and unites us with the Earth's sacred energy. It also unites us with all living things. It awakens us to our authentic human spirit; our authentic human gifts, talents, skills, and higher consciousness are revealed in our daily life. A new sense of belonging fills our sense of wellbeing. Because the river comes from the highest heavens, you will be able to breathe underwater. And when you breathe the water, the sacred water flows completely through you, healing and refreshing every part of your being. There are also flames underwater and on the surface. These are the living flames of the Holy Fire®, which do not burn but are soothing, purifying, healing, guiding, and empowering. You may have other beautiful experiences not mentioned here."

Master Class Information
If you are teaching this as part of either of the Master classes, add this information in your talk. "The River of Life Experience also gives you the ability to conduct Online Experiences and Placements or do them in person. This process is so powerful, that even if you simply read the Experiences from the book, they will work just fine. But it would be better if you practiced them until you have them memorized as it will allow you to enter the flow of the Experience better yourself."

Follow this script to present the teacher-guided portion of the Experience. Please understand that the word "Pause" in the script is not to be read to the class but is guidance for you to pause a moment to give the students time to experience what you are guiding them to do.

1. "Imagine it is a beautiful sunny day. Imagine you are barefoot walking through a beautiful forest." Pause.
2. "As you breathe into yourself, imagine you are breathing in the life essence of the forest. And with each step you take, imagine the Earth's energies are flowing up through the bottoms of your feet." Pause.
3. "As you walk along, allow yourself to experience the trees, plants, flowers and grass, and to merge with the life and the harmony and peace of the forest." Pause.
4. "As you continue to walk along, you notice that up ahead, it is getting lighter, and you realize you are coming to the edge of the forest."
5. "As you leave the forest, before you is a beautiful river. It is the River of Life. Beautiful flowers are growing along the riverbank, and there is a path following alongside the river. Follow the path alongside the river."
6. "As you walk along the path, you feel the beautiful energy of the sacred water and feel yourself becoming one with all living things." Pause.
7. "Eventually, you come to a place where you can easily enter the water. You pause at the water's edge and realize this river contains the life energy that flows through all living things. You drink from the River of Life and feel the essence of life flow through you. You realize you are one with all living things. And this gives you a sense of belonging."
8. "You enter the water completely. Feel it flowing around you."
9. "The light from the highest heavens is shining on you as you swim and float and dive into the river's depth."
10. "The River of Life is guiding you now. Allow yourself to be guided by the River of Life."

Stop talking. You can say silent prayers to Jesus, God, and the Holy Spirit. Indicate you surrender the students' experiences and yourself entirely over to them, to The Brothers and Sister of the Light, and the Ascended Masters. You can say additional prayers asking that the students receive the greatest healing and blessings God can create or other similar prayers. Then after saying prayers, direct your attention inwardly and allow yourself to be guided by the River of Life.

Using a timer or stopwatch, wait 15-25 minutes or so. Then gently bring the students back with words such as these:

1. "You can continue with your experience as long as you feel guided to do so."
2. "Whenever you are ready, take a couple of deep breaths and bring your attention to your eyes."
3. "Then, slowly open your eyes and come back."
4. After a minute, say: "Take some time to write about your experiences in your notebooks." After everyone has stopped writing, ask, "Who would like to share?"

Holy Fire® Placements I & II and Master Practitioner

When teaching Holy Fire® III Reiki classes, Placements are used instead of the attunements for Reiki I&II. Placements are done like Ignitions except they do not ignite the Holy Fire® flame inside the student. Rather, they work with the student's spirit and install Reiki energy in the student so he or she can use this energy for healing. They also activate the appropriate Reiki symbols. The Reiki energy the student receives is more refined and more effective than what was provided by attunements.

In the Placement, the teacher does not physically interact with the student. In other words, the teacher does not stand behind the student, touching the shoulders, or go to the front of the student and physically work with the hands and so forth. Instead, the teacher simply sits and guides the student in a beginning guided mediation for a few minutes, then stops talking and allows the Holy Fire® energy to administer the Placement directly to each student. Because the teacher's energy is not part of the Placement, it does not lower its vibration or affect it in any way. This allows the pure Holy Fire® energy to work in an uninhibited way. Because of this, the vibration of the Placements are much higher and the student receives higher quality healing energy.

To explain Placements to others, simply say that they are how attunements are given in Holy Fire® Reiki.

Reiki I Holy Fire® Placement
Explain the experience to your students based on the description above.

Ask the students to close their eyes and take a couple of deep breaths.

While playing soothing music in the background, follow this script:

1. "This is the Reiki I Placement. It will heal you and activate your ability to use Reiki energy."

2. "It's a beautiful day, warm and sunny. You're walking down a path in a beautiful forest. As you breathe into yourself, you breathe in the life energy of the forest and with each step that you take, you feel the energy of the earth flowing up through the bottoms of your feet."

3. "As you walk along you notice another path going off to the left. You feel compelled to follow this path."

4. "As you follow this path, you come to a clearing in the forest and in the middle of the clearing is a small hill covered with soft grass."

5. "Follow the path across to the hill and climb to the top."

6. "When you get to the top of the hill, lie down in soft grass. Feel the grass and the earth beneath your body and gaze up into the sky."

7. "Gaze up into the sky and see the beautiful white clouds. As you are gazing up at the clouds, a beautiful beam of light begins to shine down through a hole in the clouds."

8. "This is no ordinary light: it comes from the highest heaven. The light shines all around you and flows into you, filling you with warmth and feelings of safety and love."

9. "As you gaze up into the light, it begins to guide you. Follow the light."

Stop talking and wait 15-26 minutes. During this time, say this prayer: "I surrender this entire Experience to God, Jesus, Holy Spirit, and the Holy Fire®." Then simply relax enjoying the energy you are receiving.

After 15-26 minutes or so, say, "You can continue with your experience as long as you feel guided to do so." Then after waiting a short time, say, "When you are ready, take a couple of deep breaths, bring your awareness to your eyes and slowly open your eyes and return." Then after a short time say, "Take some time to write down your experiences in your notebooks."

After all have stopped writing ask students to share about their experiences.

Holy Fire® Reiki II Placement
In this Placement, use the same script as above, except let the students know this is the Reiki II Placement.

1. "This is the Reiki II Placement. It will heal you as well as upgrade your Reiki energy to Reiki II and activate the Reiki II symbols."

Follow the same script as the Reiki I Placement starting with #2.

Holy Fire® Master Practitioner Placement
This placement enhances the student's Reiki energy and activates the Usui Dai Ko Myo Master symbol fo use in Reiki sessions.

In this Placement, use the same script as for Reiki I, except let the students know this is the Master Reiki Training Placement. Substitute step #1 for the step below, then follow the other steps from the Reiki I Placement.

1. "This is the Holy Fire® Master Practitioner Placement. It will heal you, activate the Dai Ko Myo Symbol and upgrade your Reiki energy to the Reiki Master level"

Follow the same script as used for the Reiki I Placement starting with #2.

Master Ignitions

During the Master Ignitions, the Holy Fire® works with the student's spirit installing the energy and consciousness required for the student to teach and practice at the Holy Fire® III level. Once the student's spirit upgrades, it passes these changes on to the soul through an energy point below the navel. This area is usually called the lower Dantian, but it is not the same. While it is physically in a similar location as the lower Dantian, it is in a much different place energetically and exists and functions on a different level of consciousness than the Dantian system.

The Master Ignitions work on a holistic level, based on the unique energetic situation of each student. The formulation for each Ignition derives from an evaluation of the student's energy field that began the moment the student signed up for the class. Rather than the Ignitions providing the same process for each student, as is sometimes described in other Reiki systems, in the Holy Fire® system, the Ignition process is uniquely designed to create a more effective experience in harmony with the needs of each student. Because of this more nuanced process, each student can experience a higher level of transformation in a way that minimizes the discomfort and temporary imbalances sometimes experienced with Reiki attunements in the past.

After the Ignitions, the strength of the Holy Fire® energy will continue to grow over time. Its presence in your field will cause everything not in harmony with the Holy Fire® to come up for release. This release includes energies, habits, tendencies, spirit guides who have completed their work, along with any malefic spirits that may be present. However, the Holy Fire® always respects free will so for your healing and developmental processes to proceed, you must be willing to let go of these energies and entities. By allowing this to happen, more of the Holy Fire® energy will be able to function. This release will provide you with many incredible blessings including helping your life become more comfortable and more fulfilling, having more vitality and enjoyment in your life, and having your healing energies grow in strength and be more effective.

During the Ignition process, an upgrade takes place in the student's spirit in which the student gives permission for the Holy Fire® energy to interact directly with the student. This permission means that when the student becomes a teacher and conducts classes and introduces the Placement or Ignition, the energy and the experience does not flow through the teacher but goes directly to the student. This process allows higher vibrational healing energy to flow to the student than what could channel through the teacher. In the past when giving attunements, the interaction of the teacher's energy with the student actually lowered the vibration of the experience, which is why in Holy Fire® Reiki, we do not interact with the students during the Experiences, Placements and Ignitions. The teacher's energy, while helpful on some level, is lower than what the student receives directly from the Holy Fire® and the higher heavens and will interfere with what the Holy Fire® wants to give to the student. Because of this, the Experiences, Placements and Ignitions work best when the teacher doesn't intend or try to influence the Experiences, Placements or Ignitions in any way. It is best for the teacher to focus on keeping his or her energy back, close to the body during these processes, and instead say prayers of gratitude.

Procedure for the First and Second Master Ignitions
Unlike Holy Fire® II, there is no pre-Ignition in Holy Fire® III. Instead, an Ignition replaces the pre-Ignition for a total of four Ignitions. The new class outlines reflect this change. Students can sit in a circle, lay on the floor or a couch or sit in a chair as each chooses. It is also permissible for students to change their position during the Ignition process if they feel the need to do so. Meditation music can play in the background. Let the students know that they can follow your direction at the beginning, but at any time even as you continue to give guidance, they may begin being guided inwardly by the Holy Fire®. If this happens, it's okay for them to follow their inner guidance.

Script
1. Spoken slowly with appropriate pauses: "Take a deep breath and close your eyes. Bring your hands up into the Gassho position. Now focus your attention on the space between your palms. If thoughts arise in your mind, gently brush them aside and bring your attention back to the space between your palms."

2. Wait for 1–2 minutes and continue with: "A beautiful light appears high up in the heavens. The light comes down, descending all the way down to in front of your hands, then flows through your hands and into your heart. The gift of Love."

3. "The Ignition process has begin now. Remain with your eyes closed and your attention focused inwardly on your own inner experience. (Pause) Open your heart and receive as the light of your Authentic Self is revealed."

Then stop speaking and wait 20-26 minutes. During this time say prayers giving thanks for the experiences the Holy Fire® is providing to each student, and spend time going inward and being in your own experience.

Keep track of the time using a clock or cell phone set to airplane mode or use another kind of timer. When you sense it is time for the students to come back say words to this effect: "Whenever you feel ready to return, take a few breaths, bring your awareness to your eyes and slowly open your eyes and come back."

After most are back, ask them to take time to write down their experiences and to integrate.

Wait until all students finish writing, then ask, "Who would like to share his or her experience?"

Procedure for the Third and Fourth Master Ignitions

Students can lay on the floor or a couch, or sit in a chair, as each chooses. It is also permissible for students to change their position during the Ignition process if they feel the need. Meditation music can play in the background. Let the students know they can follow your direction at the beginning, but at any time, even as you continue to give guidance, they may begin being guided inwardly by the Holy Fire®. If this happens, it's okay for them to follow their inner guidance.

Follow the same Ignition process as described in the *Usui/Holy Fire® III Reiki Master Manual* (p. 93), except in the second two ignitions, substitute the numbered directions in the Master manual with these below.

1. Spoken slowly with appropriate pauses: "Take a deep breath and close your eyes. Place your palms up resting on your legs or somewhere comfortable." Pause.

2. "Focus on being receptive." Pause. "The Ignition process will begin now. Remain with your eyes closed and your attention focused inwardly on your own inner experience. **Go within, open your heart, and receive**. [Say to the students] **Say the following words to yourself, 'I am my Authentic Self.'**"

Then stop talking and wait 20-25 minutes. During this time, you can say prayers giving thanks for the experiences the Holy Fire® provides to each student, go inward, and be in your own experience.

Keep track of time. When you sense it is time for your students to come back, say, "Take as long as you like, and when you are ready to come back, bring your awareness to your eyes, then slowly open your eyes and come back. **As you come back, say to yourself, 'I am my Authentic Self.** Take this time to write about your experience and integrate."

Wait until all finish writing, then ask, "Who would like to share their experience?"

Understanding Your Ignition Experience

The Ignition process will work in many ways and on many levels. It adjusts for the individual needs of each student, whether on a conscious or unconscious level, connecting them to the formless realm. Consciously, some students may experience the Holy Fire® energy through vivid, colorful inner visions or by sensing purification processes. Other students may not have visual experiences, but instead may simply feel calm and relaxed at the same time that important healing is taking place below their level of awareness.

Conscious Level Experiences
On the conscious level, inner-vision experiences may include seeing a single flame appearing to surround one's body or sensing the installation of three flames—one in the belly, one above the head and one in the heart. Some students have reported seeing thousands of small flames appearing all over their entire body, while for others, there are no flames seen at all. The flames represent transformation points that allow the Holy Fire® energy to more easily step down from the formless realm into the world of form. Some students do not need transformation points, and the entire student's being is connected directly to the formless realm without the need for Holy Fire® flames.

Also on the conscious level, students may experience a purification process of feeling energies leaving and the Holy Fire® energy replacing them, or seeing or sensing other spiritual beings departing such as spirit guides or other entities, as they are being replaced with the Holy Fire® energy. There are many energetic experiences of this type that can take place, some of which are so new and refined that they are beyond words.

Unconscious Level Experiences
On the unconscious level, feeling calm and relaxed is just as powerful an experience and means that the energy has chosen to bypass the conscious mind and work directly with the student's core. This process is necessary for some types of deep healing because if the student is consciously aware of the process, this could lower the vibration and limit the quality of healing that takes place. This level of healing and empowerment will act like seeds that develop and grow over time, leading to feelings of having become a different and better person, without having to consciously experience the healing or transformation process that created the benefits. Because of this, many of the most significant experiences will rise to the surface of your awareness hours or days after the class is over. And in fact, the Holy Fire® experience can continue to develop and unfold for weeks or even months.

The Holy Fire® Reiki healing energy that one receives can also work in both conscious and unconscious ways when giving Holy Fire® Reiki to oneself and to others. It can feel very subtle and refined and yet create powerful effects of relaxation, well-being and healing. It can also create healing effects that are so deep, yet done in such a gentle and subtle way, that the client isn't fully aware of what has taken place until the healing that has occurred rises to the surface and it becomes apparent that important changes have taken place in one's personality. Feelings of lightness, openness and freedom, as well as new levels of peace, joy, and happiness can come welling up along with more refined feelings of love and other benefits, all of which are the result of the Holy Fire® working deeply on one's spirit.

Teaching Holy Fire® III Karuna Reiki® Classes

If you've previously taken Karuna Reiki® (the non-Holy Fire® version) and take this class, Holy Fire® III Reiki Master, you'll be able to teach both Holy Fire® III Reiki Master and Holy Fire® III Karuna Reiki®. This is because the Ignitions are done the same way in the Holy Fire® III Reiki Master class as they are done in the Holy Fire® III Karuna Reiki® class.

However, it is highly recommended that you take the Holy Fire® III Karuna Master training you haven't received within the next year or so. This is recommended as taking the class will strengthen your understanding and improve your teaching skills; more importantly, the Holy Fire® III energies and experiences are continually being upgraded and this will upgrade your Holy Fire® III Reiki energies which will benefit you and your students.

Receiving Ignitions by Yourself

After you have become a Holy Fire® III Master you can also receive additional Holy Fire® III Master Ignitions by yourself. If you would like to receive an Ignition by yourself, first say a prayer asking if it is appropriate for you to do this. If the answer is yes, in your prayer, ask what the best location and time is for you to do an Ignition by yourself. When the time comes and you are in the location you have been guided to be at for the Ignition, simply sit peacefully and draw the Holy Fire® symbol on your palms and place your hands in the gassho position. Then say a prayer asking Jesus or the Holy Spirit or the Holy Fire® to conduct the Ignition process. Look for the light in the third heaven and beyond, see it come down in front of your hands and then flow through your hands into your heart. Continue to focus your attention inwardly and follow the light.

Holy Fire® III Reiki and Spiritual Guidance

Spiritual guidance can come from many sources that vary in quality and benefit. The section on the Twelve Heavens on page 27 explains this more clearly. Sometimes the spirit guides people have connected with come from the second heaven or are using a combination of second and third heaven energies. Because of this, the quality of the guidance and help they provide isn't as useful as it could be. One of the things that the Ignition process does is to release spirits and guides that are not compatible with the development of Holy Fire® consciousness. This usually involves a situation in which the guide has a connection to second heaven energies. This process of purification can also continue with other experiences in class and can also continue after class.

As you've read in other sections of the manual, the purpose of spirit guides is to guide you to the Source and then help you develop a stronger connection with the Source. If this is to happen the guides must have a strong, clear, and exclusive connection with Holy Fire® consciousness. The Holy Fire® originates in the higher heavens and can provide you with a direct connection to the Source. Because of this, the Holy Fire® is able to discern which guides are supportive of your development and which are not. And then with your permission, and in a respectful way, it will release those guides that can no longer help you. Please see the section on page 32, The Brothers and Sisters of the Light, for more information on this subject.

As this process progresses, you will be provided with a very clear and beneficial form of guidance. And as this process unfolds, you'll enter into a higher and more refined state of consciousness in which you'll experience Divine Revelation. This means you are being guided directly by the Source, by God. This is a truly wonderful experience that feels as though you have come home. The guidance you receive will include a feeling of certainty. This will give you confidence and help you live your life with the feeling that you are on a safe and beneficial journey that is healthy for you, your family, and others in your life.

In addition to receiving guidance, you will also receive the personal qualities and energies necessary to follow the guidance. This could include confidence, physical energy and vitality, clarity of mind and purpose, and many other qualities. You'll find it easy to make effective plans or be guided to simply start your project knowing you'll be guided along the way. The guidance will also include love. This is a special love that is very healing and nurturing, and that reaches out to all those you interact with as you carry out what you are guided to do. This will make it easy for people to want to help you and make your projects a blessing for them too.

You are on a journey to discover wonderful resources that have been waiting to help you. These gifts are available to you because you are loved by the Source and the gifts are an expression of this love. It is hoped by the Source that you'll accept them and by doing so, you will recognize that you are loved.

Editors Note: Please be aware that there can be enlightened beings and other beings in the second heaven that have a very high level of consciousness. However, these beings are not from the second heaven but dwell there to help the majority of spirits in the second heaven. The spirits referred to as coming from the second heaven are those who are limited to the second heaven and are not able to go any higher. These spirits have unhealed egos and it is the second heaven where potentially harmful spirits are located.

Maintain and Develop Your Holy Fire® Energy

Your connection with the Holy Fire® is valuable and will provide you with many benefits which include experiences of joy, peace, love, happiness, abundance, healing, guidance, empowerment and even more than this. In order to maintain your Holy Fire® connection and make use of its benefits and develop the energy even further, it's important to use the energy regularly, share it with others and practice as many of the following activities as you are able to do.

1. Give yourself Holy Fire® Reiki sessions every day.

2. Receive Holy Fire® Reiki sessions from others.

3. Give Holy Fire® Reiki sessions to others.

4. Practice Holy Fire® Meditation.

5. Pray to Jesus, the Holy Spirit, God, the Holy Fire® or other enlightened beings you are familiar with, asking for guidance and saying this prayer: "Guide me and heal me so that I might be of greater service to myself and to others."

6. Receive Ignitions by yourself as explained above.

7. Teach Holy Fire® Reiki classes.

Holy Fire® energy comes from an unlimited supply. This means that not only can it provide you and everyone on the planet with an abundance of it's amazing benefits, but the quality of the benefits can improve as well. There is no limit to how deeply and completely it can heal or to the quality of life it can help you experience. Therefore, I encourage you to make use of this wonderful gift.

Class Outlines

The following class outlines are made available for your use. These are the class outlines used by the members of the Reiki Membership Association and by our Licensed Reiki Master Teachers. The outlines combine the Western style of Reiki with the Japanese style and Holy Fire® III Reiki. The Reiki I & II outlines are made to be used with the *Reiki, The Healing Touch* class manual, which includes instruction on how to do all the techniques in the outlines including the Japanese Reiki Techniques (JRT). You may also want to get a copy of the Japanese Reiki Techniques workshop DVD, which will instruct you on how to practice all the Japanese Reiki Techniques. The Reiki Master and Reiki Master Class outlines are to be used with this manual. These outlines are downloadable from our website. Give each student a copy of the class manual when they sign up, and a copy of the symbols if they are part of the class, so they can memorize them. Explain the private nature of the symbols and that they should not share them with others.

Usui/Holy Fire® III Class Outlines

Usui/Holy Fire® III
Reiki I Training
Suggested class time: 9 a.m.–6:30 p.m.

1. Registration and sign in.
2. Smudging or energy clearing. Have students raise hands and place positive energy all over the room and then get hugs from everyone.
3. Introductions—name, where you are from, why you decided to take this class and something you like about yourself.
4. Ocean of Holy Love Experience. Have students write experiences and share.
5. Reiki Talk—what is Rei-ki, the different levels, how the Placement process works. How does Reiki work? (Use information from the manual.) For what can it be used? (Use examples and Reiki stories to explain these topics.) History–Usui–Hayashi–Takata–22 Masters and include information on the Gakkai and the discovery of the Japanese Reiki Techniques and a brief history of the Holy Fire®.
6. Explain and review the Reiki Ideals. Explain that the Reiki energy in this class is based on the Usui/Holy Fire® III system.
7. Lunch (one hour).
8. Return and regroup—circle shoulder massages and hugs.
9. Explain Gassho meditation (page 56, *Reiki: The Healing Touch*).
10. Briefly explain the three heavens and talk about the Placement and how it works.
11. Reiki I Placement.
12. Have students write about the Placement and experiences then share.
13. Break (10 minutes).
14. Practice Reiki (three or four to a group)—make sure all feel Reiki or that the client does. Share after.
15. Byosen Scanning (page 57, *Reiki: The Healing Touch*)—pick a partner, scan, then switch. Explain Reiji-ho (page 56, *Reiki: The Healing Touch*) and that it is more advanced as one uses intuition directly rather than the hand.
16. Explain and practice the standard session for treating others, all hand positions (pick a partner and switch).
17. Explain and demonstrate Kenyoku (page 61, *Reiki: The Healing Touch*). Have students use it at the end of the session.
18. Explain Hayashi Healing Guide and how to use it.
19. Explain the Reiki Client Information Form, Reiki Documentation Form and charging money or bartering.
20. Go over the Code of Ethics and Standards of Practice.
21. Break (10 to 15 minutes).
22. Explain self-session—Byosen self-scan (page 60, *Reiki: The Healing Touch*) and practice self-session hand positions.
23. *If students are continuing the next day: Reiki II Symbols—show for memorization only, sacred, keep them secret, explain the test. Distribute handout. (Use last 1/2 hour of class for this part.) If students are taking Reiki II, it's a good idea to give each a copy of the Reiki II symbols when they sign up, so they have time to memorize them.
24. Closing meditation or prayer.

Usui/Holy Fire® III
Reiki II Training
Suggested class time: 9 a.m.–6:30 p.m.

1. Registration. Smudging or energy clearing. Place Reiki all over the room and then get hugs from everyone. Do introductions if this class is taught separately from Reiki I—name, where you are from, why you decided to take this class and something you like about yourself.
2. Holy Love Experience. Have students write experiences in notebooks and share.
3. Talk on Reiki II symbols—deeper, complete meaning, how to use them including the many ways to use Hon Sha Ze Sho Nen for distant and past/future healing. Explain why they need to be kept private as described on page 47 of *Reiki: The Healing Touch*. Explain that the energy in this class is based on the Usui/Holy Fire® III system.
4. Lunch (one hour). Students can use some of the lunchtime to memorize the symbols.
5. Test on symbols—use the form on page 165 of the *Usui/Holy Fire® III Reiki Master Manual*. Make copies for your students. If there are errors, gently point them out and ask the student to correct them. Use hints if necessary or have the person use her notes. Coach so that everyone passes.
6. Circle massages and hugs.
7. Explain Placement. Conduct a Reiki II Placement.
8. Have students write Placement experiences in their notebooks—sharing.
9. Break (10 minutes).
10. Break up into groups of three to four to practice. Start with them doing straight Reiki without any symbols. Then have them add the Choku Rei and after five minutes or so, share how this felt. Repeat with the Sei heki, so they get an experience of what the symbols do while in class.
11. Explain how to do a complete session using all the symbols.
12. Practice Gyoshi-ho (page 62, *Reiki: The Healing Touch*)—choose partners and switch. You can do this exercise with the students sitting in two rows of chairs facing each other. Also, explain that a practitioner can use this in a regular session. (Note that this replaces Beaming.)
13. Enkaku chiryo (page 62, *Reiki: The Healing Touch*) with the group. Ask for requests from students. Write the names of those to whom you are sending Reiki on a piece of paper and place in the middle of the circle or use a photo of the person if it is available. Send to create harmony among all people on the planet or perhaps a world situation.
14. Have students pick a Reiki buddy to exchange Reiki with during the week and to send distant Reiki to and then share the experience.
15. Ending meditation or prayer.
16. Encourage students to participate in a Reiki support group.

Usui/Holy Fire® III
Reiki Master Class

Suggested class time: 9 a.m.–6:30 p.m.
This outline is for teaching the 3-day Reiki Master class.

Day 1
1. Registration and sign in.
2. Smudging or energy clearing. Place Reiki all over the room and then get hugs from everyone.
3. Introductions—name, work, family, metaphysical background, understanding of Reiki, why you want to learn Reiki, and something you like about yourself.
4. Explain our definition of Soul and Spirit and the Heavens. Explain that the energy in this class is based on the Usui/Holy Fire® III system.
5. Explain the unique way that Holy Fire® III Experiences, Placements and Ignitions are done. Explain that in this class students will not learn how to give attunements in the usual way, and that Holy Fire® attunements are called Placements. Placements are given for Reiki I and II and the first part of Master and provide a stronger, more effective healing energy for the student, open students to higher consciousness and activate the symbol(s). Explain how Holy Fire® III works and the concepts of the Authentic Self, the Culturally-Created Self and the Dormant Self.
6. Explain that when teaching Online classes, the class outlines in the Online section are used.
7. Healing in the River of Life Experience Introduction: Use script on page 89 of the Usui/Holy Fire® III Reiki Master Manual to explain the River of Life Experience. Explain that at the same time this experience will be a healing experience, it will also give the students the ability to give Placements for Reiki I&II and to empower the Usui Master symbol in the Reiki Master class.
8. Healing in the River of Life Experience, have students write experiences and share.
9. Using crystals and stones with Reiki—how to use a single crystal to send Reiki continuously. Making a Reiki grid that will continue to send Reiki to yourself and others: used for distant healing, personal healing, goals, and manifestation. Note, this step can be done later in the day or on the second day if you don't have time.
10. The Usui Dai Ko Myo—show it to students, explain usage, practice drawing it. Go over the meaning of the Japanese words and explain what it means to Reiki people. Do the same with the Holy Fire® symbol.
11. Lunch (one hour). Use some of the lunchtime to memorize the symbols if needed.
12. Test on both symbols.
13. Explain how Placements work; that they do not come from the teacher or through the teacher but come to the student directly from the Holy Fire®.
14. Conduct the Master Practitioner Placement. Have students write down their experiences and share.

15. Break (10 minutes.)
16. Explain the Ignition process and that you will give a brief guided meditation and then stop talking while the energy guides the student directly. Explain that some students may have inner experiences, and some may just feel relaxed and that the most important effects take place below the students' level of awareness. Explain that the four Ignitions empower the Holy Fire® symbol in a wholistic, non-liner way.
17. Conduct the first ignition. Give students time to write down their experiences and to share with the group.
18. Break (10 minutes).
19. Practice with both symbols. Break up into groups of 3-4 students per Reiki table. Have students draw the Usui Master symbol on their hands and practice with this symbol for 6-8 minutes or so. Then have them draw the Holy Fire® symbol on their hands and practice with this symbol for 6-8 minutes or so. Then have the receiver share with their group what the energy of each symbol felt like. Then go on to the the next student in the group until all have received and shared.
20. Come back into the class circle and ask students to share their experience of the Usui Master symbol and the Holy Fire® symbol.
21. Reiki Moving Meditation. This exercise can be covered now or the next day Use the Holy Fire® symbol.

Day 2
1. Registration.
2. Smudging or energy clearing. Place Reiki all over the room and then get hugs from everyone.
3. Second Ignition. Give students time to write down their experiences and to share.
4. Explain the evolution of Reiki and how it developed from Usui Reiki into Holy Fire® Reiki.
5. Describe the history of Holy Fire® Reiki.
6. Describe the essence of Reiki.
7. Holy Fire® Symbol—show students, explain the attributes and benefits and usage, practice drawing it. Test on the symbol. You can also do this as part of step #11 on the first day of the Reiki Master class.
8. Explain Holy Fire® III Reiki and spiritual guidance.
9. Lunch (one hour).
10. Third Ignition. Follow instructions. Have students write experiences in notebooks, then share.
11. Practice giving Reiki sessions using Holy Fire®. Three students giving Reiki to one.
12. Break (10 to 15 minutes).
13. Holy Fire® Healing Experience. Follow instructions on page 87 of the *Usui/Holy Fire® III Reiki Master Manual* and have students choose two things they would like to have completely healed and so forth. Then conduct the Holy Fire® Healing Experience. Have students share their experiences.
14. If you have extra time, you could do one of the Holy Love Experiences.
15. Questions and Answers.

Day 3
1. Smudging or energy clearing. Place Reiki energy all over the room, then give hugs to each other.
2. Fourth Ignition. Follow instructions. Have students write experiences in notebooks, then share.
3. Discussion—the values and spiritual orientation of a true Reiki Master.
4. Questions and Answers or discuss other Holy Fire® concepts.
5. Lunch (one hour).
6. Practice Reiki in groups of three to four using Holy Fire®. Seven minutes per student or longer.
7. Explain how to practice Holy Fire® Meditation. Practice it if you have time.
8. Explain healing religious trauma.
9. If you have time, talk about the Brothers and Sisters of the light, Unification Consciousness, Becoming the Authentic Self and The Spirit of the Earth.
10. Explain Healing Spirit Attachments. Conduct this process for the class if you have time.
11. Experiences, Placements, and Ignitions—go over the outlines, discuss, explain how to do them. Practice is usually not needed.
12. Conduct another of the Holy Love Experiences if you have time.
13. Talk about teaching, go over class outlines.
14. Explain doing Ignitions by yourself.
15. Go over the Code of Ethics and Standards of Practice.
16. Talk about developing your Reiki practice and the value of membership in the Reiki Membership Association (RMA).
17. Pass out class review.
18. Pass out student certificates.
19. Closing prayer.

Holy Fire® III Karuna Reiki® Master Class

Day 1
1. Registration.
2. Smudging or another form of energy clearing.
3. Send Reiki to four directions—sky and ground and all around the classroom.
4. Get a hug from each person and welcome each to the class.
5. Introductions—name, where you are from, why you decided to take this class and something you like about yourself.
6. Explain our definition of Soul and Spirit, the Heavens and Letting Go of Guides. Explain that the Reiki energy in this class is based on the Usui/Holy Fire® III system.
7. Explain the unique way that Holy Fire® III Experiences, Placements and Ignitions are done. Explain that in this class four Ignitions are given. The four Ignitions activate the nine symbols of this class and give the student the ability to give Ignitions. Also explain that after this class, when teaching Reiki I&II and when activating the Usui Master symbol in Reiki Master, Placements will be given instead of attunements. Placements and Ignitions are easier to do and provide a stronger and more effective experience than attunements. Also explain the concepts of the Authentic Self, the Culturally Created Self and the Dormant Self.
8. Explain that when teaching Online classes, the class outlines in the Online section are used.
9. Healing in the River of Life introduction. Explain how it works; is a healing experience and sets up the ability to give Placements for use when teaching Usui/Holy Fire® Reiki for I and II and Usui/Holy Fire® Master.
10. Healing in the River of Life Experience, have students write experiences and share.
11. Break.
12. Brief history of Reiki including the idea that Reiki has evolved with Usui, Hayashi and Takata and there is no limit to the quantity and quality of Reiki that is possible for us to channel.
13. Explain Holy Fire® III Karuna Reiki® including origin. Explain Holy Fire® III Reiki and spiritual guidance.
14. Lunch.
15. Explain that the class is both a practitioner and master class and that the master Ignitions both initiate the student as a Karuna Master with the ability to teach and give Ignitions and attunes the student to each of the practitioner symbols for use in sessions. Because of this, only Ignitions are given to the student by the teacher in this class and that there are four.
16. Explain how they will be able to teach all their classes as Holy Fire® classes including I and II, Usui/Holy Fire® Master and Karuna and that the Holy Fire® Placements for Usui/Holy Fire® I and II and Master will be explained in class.
17. Explain how Ignitions work and that they do the same thing as attunements. Explain that you will give a brief guided meditation and then stop talking while the energy guides the student directly. Explain that some students may have inner

experiences, and some may simply feel relaxed and that the most important effects take place below the students' level of awareness. Explain that the four Ignitions work holistically to empower all nine Karuna symbols and this process works in a unique way for each student.

18. Do first Ignition with integration time and sharing.
19. Break.
20. Tell students about the Holy Fire® symbol and energy.
21. Show them how to draw the symbol. Have them practice drawing it if they haven't already memorized it.
22. Talk about each of the Karuna I symbols, how to draw them and what they are used for and go over them thoroughly.
23. Test on the Holy Fire® symbol and the Karuna I symbols.
24. Break.
25. Talk about the Karuna II symbols, how to draw them and what they are used for and go over them thoroughly.
26. Test on the Karuna II symbols. An alternate method is to teach all nine symbols at the same time and give one test for all of them.
27. Ending prayer or affirmation. Hugs.

Day 2
1. Smudging or other energy clearing process, energy sent around the room, hugs.
2. Ask students to share how they are experiencing the class and if they have any questions or comments.
3. Second Ignition.
4. Break.
5. Talk about the trademark for Holy Fire® III Karuna Reiki® and why it was developed.
6. Lunch.
7. Do the third Ignition. Write experiences and share.
8. Break.
9. Practice using the Holy Fire® and Karuna I symbols starting with the Holy Fire® symbol and using each of the four Karuna I practitioner symbols, three to four students at each table. Practice each symbol for approximately 5-7 minutes or so. After each student finishes, have the client share the feeling of each symbol with their group. Also, ask each person in the group to share what it was like to use the energy.
10. Experiences, Placements and Ignitions, explain how these are done and go over the scripts. Practice is usually not needed.
11. Explain Holy Fire® III Meditation and practice if you have time.
12. End class with prayer, affirmation or hugs.

Day 3

1. Smudging or other energy clearing process, energy sent around the room, hugs.
2. Ask students to share how they are experiencing the class and if they have any questions or comments.
3. Do the fourth Ignition. Write experiences and share.
4. Go over all the class outlines for all levels. Talk about how the teacher needs to keep his or her energy out of the Experiences, Placements and Ignitions and how these are done without the teacher physically interacting with the students. Furthermore, the teacher does not hold space or intend, but instead, focuses on keeping his or her energy back from the students and held close to the teacher's body. Explain that this allows the energies to go directly to the student without being slowed or affected by the teacher and that this keeps the energy pure and allows it to be more powerful and effective. However, the teacher can pray directly to God, Source, Creator etc. praying for the benefit of the students and asking that God's will for each student be fully manifest.
5. Additional topics can be covered such as the World Peace Reiki Grid project or the benefits of the RMA, or the Center for Reiki Research.
6. Lunch.
7. Practice Holy Fire® and the Karuna II symbols same as step #9 from the previous day. Decide on the time used for each symbol based on the remaining class time. You could also combine this step with Chanting done as the last part with each client on the table rather than presenting it separately in #9. If you do this, use step #10 to explain the difference between Chanting and Toning.
8. Break.
9. Chanting and toning. Practice chanting unless you practiced it in step #7. If you have time, you can practice toning or demonstrate it. An alternative method to practice chanting is to have students write the name of a person on a piece of paper and place it on the altar in the center of the circle. Then have the students draw one or more Karuna symbols on their hands and hold them facing the altar as the group chants the name of the Karuna symbol(s) together using one symbol at a time.
10. Explain the importance of releasing negative spirits and explain the Healing Spirit Attachment process. Conduct this exercise for the whole class if you have time.
11. Cover anything remaining to be covered and ask for final questions.
12. Pass out class review.
13. Graduation—pass out certificates.
14. Final prayer or affirmation.
15. Hugs.

Holy Fire® III Upgrade Class

Those who are Holy Fire® III Reiki Masters can teach this class. Only those who already are Holy Fire® or Holy Fire® II Reiki Masters can take it. It requires approximately 3-4 hours to teach and will upgrade qualified students to the Holy Fire® III level for either Usui/Holy Fire® Reiki or Holy Fire® Karuna Reiki®. Please note that the reason William could teach this class as a webinar is that he received many sessions with Jesus to upgrade his energy field to be able to do it and therefore had the permission and participation of Jesus when doing the webinars. Because of this, it is important that you present this webinar in person to your students.

Topics
1. Review the history of Holy Fire® Reiki.
2. Review the philosophy and the central ideas of Holy Fire® Reiki.
3. Briefly review the history of Usui Reiki focusing on how Usui Sensei's instruction specified that the most important activity for a Reiki practitioner is to continually seek to develop one's ability to channel ever higher frequencies of Reiki energy.
4. Explain Placements and how they replace the attunements for Reiki I and II and ART. Also, explain how to conduct them.
5. Explain the Upgrade Ignition and how it will upgrade one's Holy Fire® energy to Holy Fire® III.
6. Conduct the Upgrade Ignition.
7. Practice giving Holy Fire® III Reiki to each other with several students giving Reiki to one student and then switching, so each student receives a session. Session time could be between 15-20 minutes each or longer if time allows. Ask students to share among their group about their experiences after each person receives Reiki.
8. Go over the class outlines for Holy Fire® III Reiki classes.
9. Review how to present the Experiences and the Ignitions.
10. Have a question-and-answer session answering questions students may have about teaching Holy Fire® III classes or giving sessions or any other questions students may have about Reiki.
11. Close with prayers or affirmations, giving thanks for the gift of Holy Fire® Reiki and asking the Source of Reiki to guide and bless the students and their clients.

Giving a Holy Fire® Reiki Talk
This outline can also be used at a Reiki share group or a Reiki session.

A Holy Fire® Reiki Talk as outlined here is more than just a talk as it includes a Holy Fire® Experience. Hosted by a Holy Fire® Reiki Master, it is an easy and enjoyable way for people to be introduced to Holy Fire® Reiki and to actually experience its healing energy.

Promotion
Hard copy flyers can be created and posted on bulletin boards, announcements can be made on Facebook, on your web site, and sent by email directing people back to your web site announcement, and also by word of mouth.

Location
It could be held at a home, an auditorium, or a conference room.

Fee
It could be free or a small fee could be charged to cover expenses.

Outline
1. Could be a similar set up as for a Reiki circle or share group.
2. Arrive at the meeting room early and say prayers and become receptive to the Holy Fire® energy asking it to clear the room of any energies not compatible with Holy Fire® and to bless the room.
3. Registration could be done with hard copy forms or with a computer form set up for people to fill out. Minimum information would be the person's name and email address.
4. When people arrive, allow them to mill and talk.
5. Then ask them to sit. If it's a smaller group, do introductions – name, where are you from, if they have Reiki or not. Then ask them to stand and with permission share hugs. If it's a larger group in an auditorium, have them stand and introduce themselves to 3 people, then get 3 hugs and sit down.
6. Brief talk on what is Reiki.
7. Explain the evolution of Reiki and how it developed from Usui Reiki into Holy Fire® Reiki.
8. Describe the qualities of Holy Fire® Reiki.
9. If there are people present who have Holy Fire® Reiki, ask if any of them would like to describe their experience of Holy Fire® Reiki.
10. Questions and Answers.
11. Break
12. Talk about the Holy Fire® Reiki Experience and how it works. That you'll be conducting a brief guided meditation and then stop talking for about 20 min. during which time the Holy Fire® energy will be working directly with each person, providing a unique healing experience that contains what is needed by each person. Also explain that some will experience inner experiences such as

seeing colors or feeling waves of healing energy flowing through them or visions of spiritual beings and so forth, and that others will simply feel relaxed, but that everyone will receive something important that will continue to produce benefits even after the event.
13. Conduct the Holy Love Experience or the Ocean of Holy Love Experience, the Heavenly Banquet Hall Experience, or the Holy Fire® Healing Experience. Play Julie True, Music to Journal by Vol 1 or other similar music.
14. After bringing people back, ask them to write down their experiences, then share if they choose to do so.
15. Close with a prayer or positive affirmation.

Notes

Chanting & Toning

Our experience with Holy Fire® III Karuna Reiki® has taught us that toning or chanting during a Holy Fire® III Karuna Reiki® session creates profound shifts in the vibrational frequency of the healing energy. When chanting and toning, we encourage you to do it out loud when appropriate. However, you can chant or tone telepathically as well. When chanting or toning in groups of three or more, it is important not to chant or tone for longer than 15 minutes altogether.

Chanting
We define chanting as sounding the name of the symbol, or the sound of a series of symbols with your Karuna Reiki® empowered voice, so as to enhance the overall qualities of Karuna Reiki® while your hands are on or near the recipient's body. The energies will guide themselves going to the place they are needed.

Toning
We define toning as sounding the name of the symbol with your Karuna Reiki® empowered voice, while your hands are a few inches to a few feet from the client, beaming Karuna Reiki® into a specific area in need of healing. The purpose is to direct the energy directly into a block or area in need of healing.

It is permissible to chant or tone the names of the Karuna symbols with clients who have not taken Karuna Reiki® training, just don't show them what the symbols look like. If they ask you what you are chanting or toning, simply tell them that they are healing sounds.

When one allows oneself to truly channel the chanting and toning sounds, it can improve one's overall ability to channel healing energy. This technique can take us to higher levels of consciousness and invite new guides to help and to channel through us in exciting and powerful ways.

Before beginning the chanting or toning, empower your hands by drawing the Karuna Reiki® Master symbols and the other symbols you will be using on your hands. Then place one hand at your heart center and one hand on your throat, applying Karuna Reiki® for a few minutes, and then place both hands on your throat. As you do this, silently chant one or more of the Karuna Reiki® symbols. As the Karuna Reiki® is flowing, focus on preparing yourself to channel Karuna Reiki® with your voice, releasing any fears or insecurities and also any judgement or expectations of yourself or others that might exist concerning chanting or singing aloud for others to hear. Then attune to the Source of Karuna Reiki® and the purest spiritual guides. In a prayer ask for the perfect healing to take place and intend to serve as a pure and open channel for the Karuna Reiki® energy to flow through.

Chanting and toning for healing is different than singing. Occasionally chants or tones which may sound off key to us may be exactly what the recipient needs. It is our responsibility to be open and trust the infinite intelligence of Karuna to guide the process. Chanting and toning with Karuna Reiki® is another form of channeling healing energy, it doesn't always sound like we might think it should if we analyze it, but if we truly offer ourselves as pure and open channels and allow the sound to resonate from our hearts, beautiful healing will flow forth in the form of sound.

Chanting & Toning with Holy Fire® III Karuna Reiki®

Chanting the Holy Fire® III Karuna Reiki® symbols can be added at any time during a regular Reiki® Karuna session. The below chants can be done as described or you can add the Holy Fire® symbol to the beginning of each chant.

Examples

At the beginning of a session place your hands on the sides of the client's head, chant Zonar seven times, pause and allow the energy to flow. This intensifies the energy flow through the crown and higher chakras, while creating a protective shell around all the energy bodies retaining the healing energies and allowing them to penetrate more deeply. Then give a normal Holy Fire® III Karuna Reiki® session as guided.

After giving Holy Fire® III Karuna Reiki® to a client in this manner, repeat the above technique except instead of chanting Zonar, chant Rama seven times. This assists in releasing negative energies, and balances the upper and lower chakra energies. Next chant Halu, Harth, Halu (three times), then Zonar, Rama, Zonar (three times). This completes the releasing process, fills the aura with an energy of compassion for self and others, and seals the session in a glow of unconditional love and peace. This can also be done with hands on the feet.

Place your hands on the sides of the client's head, chant Halu three times, then Kriya three times, then Rama three times, pause and allow the energy to flow. This technique sends a powerful stream of high frequency Holy Fire® III Karuna Reiki® energy down through the crown, all the way through the energy system and out the feet, clearing blockages to fulfilling one's spiritual purpose, and anchoring them to that purpose and the earth. Clairvoyantly this appears as a pillar of iridescent white light, shooting with great intensity through the energy system, and all energy bodies.

Pain or tension. Place your hands on an area of pain or tension, chant Zonar, Harth, Rama three times, pause and allow the energy to flow. Continue as many times as needed.

This technique relieves pain, and muscular tension or muscle spasms.

With recipient sitting upright, place hands at back of neck, with thumbs placed on the indentation at the base of the skull (the mouth of God) and chant Iava (Eeeeee-aaaaaa-vaa) three times.

This technique fills the crown first with a velvety black light, and the sensation of a crown being placed on the head and then shifts to a deep, but brilliant, indigo blue light, which then flows through the entire body. This promotes visual clarity, increases the frequency of light around the recipient and practitioner, and assists one in staying focused on their highest purpose, and to fully experience and remain in the moment.

Additional chants that work well
Zonar-Iava-Gnosa, Shanti-Shanti-Rama, Halu-Halu-Harth, Gnosa-Harth-Shanti, Gnosa-Kriya-Gnosa, Halu-Harth-Shanti. Go ahead and experiment with other combinations. You are sure to find some great ones!

These are just a few examples of ways you can use chanting, and different symbol combinations to generate more effective healing results.

We are continuously researching new techniques, and encourage all Karuna Reiki® Practitioners to do so.

Toning with Holy Fire® III Karuna Reiki®

Your voice can be empowered by Holy Fire® III Karuna Reiki® and used during a session. It is especially useful in releasing blocks and negative energy.

1. Scan the person to locate the area of concern. You can also use the technique used in aura clearing, which is taught in the ART class, to help the person locate the problem, asking them to find the location of the cause, shape, color, sound, weight, etc.
2. Once the area is located, meditate on the area and pray to the Higher Power, asking the Holy Fire® III Karuna Reiki® symbol that is right for treating this area to come in to your mind. Then empower your hands by drawing this symbol on each hand and clapping them together three times as you say the name of the symbol to yourself three times.
3. Then place one hand at your heart center and one hand on your throat, applying Holy Fire® III Karuna Reiki® for a few minutes, and then place both hands on your throat. As you do this, silently chant the Holy Fire® III Karuna Reiki® symbol you have been guided to use. As Holy Fire® III Karuna Reiki® is flowing, focus on preparing yourself to channel Holy Fire® III Karuna Reiki® with your voice, releasing any fears or insecurities, and also any judgement or expectations of yourself or others, that might exist concerning toning aloud for others to hear.
4. Say a prayer asking that Holy Fire® energy to work with you.
5. Draw the Holy Fire® III Karuna Reiki® symbol you will be using over the area of concern on the client.
6. With your hands placed several inches, to several feet from the client, begin beaming Holy Fire® III Karuna Reiki® to the area.

7. Take a deep breath and begin toning out loud. Use a long continuous tone that resonates on each vowel.
8. As you tone, direct your hands toward the area of concern intending that you are sending Reiki with your hands, also stare intently at the area intending that you are sending Reiki with your eyes.
9. You will be using both your Holy Fire® III Karuna Reiki® empowered eyes, your voice, and your Holy Fire® III Karuna Reiki® hands at the same time.
10. Continue to tone until you feel that the block is gone. Then ask the client how they feel and what is happening in the area - get feedback. Re-scan the area to see if additional toning is necessary and to feel the results of your work.
11. You may be guided to tone other Holy Fire® III Karuna Reiki® symbols.
12. Follow with Usui or Holy Fire® III Karuna Reiki® to the area and follow your inner guidance in knowing how to complete the session.

Toning is a very powerful technique that amplifies the Holy Fire® III Karuna Reiki® energies and sends them even deeper into the client's body and energy field.

ICRT Reiki Membership Association
Code of Ethics

1. **Confidentiality:** No information about the client will be disclosed to any third party without the written consent of the client or the parent or guardian if the client is under 18.

2. **Transparency:** Include on your website and be willing to explain to prospective clients or students your training background, what takes place in a Reiki session, the subjects covered in your classes, the amount of time spent in sessions and classes and the fee charged.

3. **Integrity:** Be honest in all your activities and communication.

4. **Support:** Have a friendly, positive regard toward your clients and students and openly encourage them to heal and to do the best job possible with their Reiki practice and/or teaching program.

5. **Respect:** Value your clients and students and treat them with respect. Never engage in any illegal or immoral activity with your clients or students. Never touch their genital area or breasts, never ask them to disrobe, and never make sexual comments, jokes or references. Abstain from the use of drugs or alcohol during all professional activities.

6. **Honor:** Honor all Reiki practitioners and teachers regardless of lineage or organizational affiliation. Refrain from making negative statements about other Reiki practitioners or teachers.

7. **Educate:** Inform your clients and student about the value of Reiki sessions and that they do not provide a cure and are not a substitute for care by a licensed health care provider.

8. **Refer:** Acknowledge that Reiki works in conjunction with other forms of medical or psychological care. If a client or student has a medical or psychological condition, suggest, in addition to giving them Reiki sessions, they see a licensed health care provider.

9. **Non-Interference:** Never diagnose medical or psychological conditions or prescribe medications. Never suggest that a client change or end dosages of substances prescribed by other licensed health care providers or suggest the client change prescribed treatment or interfere with the treatment of a licensed health care provider.

10. **Honesty:** Never use another person's copyrighted material in your classes, website or literature without permission and giving credit.

11. **Freedom:** Encourage your students to use their own inner guidance in determining who to take classes from including the possibility of studying with more than one teacher.

12. **Professional Conduct:** Always act in such a way so as to create and maintain a professional image for the practice of Reiki and for the ICRT Reiki Membership Association.

13. **Development:** Be involved in the continuing process of healing yourself on all levels so as to fully express the essence of Reiki in all you do. Be in agreement with and working to fully express the Usui Ideals and the ICRT Center Philosophy.

14. **Gratitude:** Be grateful for the gift of Reiki and for each client and student who chooses to come to you.

ICRT Reiki Membership Association
Standards of Practice

1. Use ICRT manuals when teaching your classes. Supply one manual per student. Manuals must be purchased from www.reikiwebstore.com.

2. Professional members: supply the RMA certificates for your students.

3. Professional members use the title of Professional member of the RMA or Professional member of the Reiki Membership Association in their advertising and literature. Affiliate members use the title of Affiliate member of the RMA or Affiliate member of the Reiki Membership Association in their advertising and literature.

4. Reply to all Reiki related e-mail and voice mail in a timely way.

5. Use a client information form and session documentation form in your Reiki sessions (available on website under Resources and Downloads).

6. Create a safe, comfortable, harmonious space for your sessions and classes.

7. Training including Attunements, Placements and Ignitions may be given in person or online.

8. When teaching Reiki classes, use only the RMA Reiki symbols as drawn by Mrs. Takata for Reiki II, the Master Practitioner symbol and the Holy Fire® symbol for Reiki Master which are in the Reiki Master manual. No symbols are taught in Reiki I.

9. Include time for lecture, discussion, demonstration, practice time and questions and answers in all your classes.

10. Reiki I & II can be taught together (Hayashi style) or separately according to teacher preference.

11. In the Usui/Holy Fire® classes, ART and Master are now being taught together as one class called Reiki Master while in the Usui/Tibetan style, ART and Master are still taught separately or together as one class.

12. Require that a student have practiced at the Reiki II level for a minimum of six months before taking ART or Reiki Master.

13. Use the RMA class outlines. Additional topics can be taught at teacher's discretion.

14. Minimum class times. The lower number is for small classes of 1-3 students and the longer time is for larger classes.
    Reiki I – 5-8 hours
    Reiki II – 5-8 hours
    Usui/Tibetan ART – 5-8 hours
    Usui/Tibetan Master – 10-16 hours
    Usui/Tibetan Art/Master – 15-24 hours
    Usui/Holy Fire® Reiki Master – 15-24 hours

Minimum Teaching Requirements

1. Use the same Holy Fire® III Karuna Reiki® symbols taught by The International Center for Reiki Training and that appear in the ICRT Holy Fire® III Karuna Reiki® manuals.

2. Use the same Holy Fire® III Karuna Reiki® Ignitions taught by The International Center for Reiki Training and that appear in the ICRT Holy Fire® III Karuna Reiki® manuals. The Ignitions must be done in person. Distant Ignitions for initiation purposes are not part of the Karuna Reiki® program. For further information, please see the article on distant attunements on our web site, www.reiki.org.

3. Use the Holy Fire® III Karuna Reiki® manual(s) offered by the Center as your class manual and provide one for each student. You must purchase these manuals from the Center or from one of our representatives - no photocopying is allowed. These manuals are sold at a discounted price to Registered teachers when purchased in lots of five or more of the same title.

4. Explain the Holy Fire® III Karuna Reiki® trademark information to students.

5. Teach the following subjects:
    a. Describe the history of Holy Fire® III Karuna Reiki® as described in the manual.
    b. Describe how to draw each symbol and have each student memorize them.
    c. Describe how to activate the symbols.
    d. Describe the uses of each symbol.
    e. Give the Center Ignition for each level taught.
    f. Provide practice time in the use of each symbol.
    g. Explain how to do Placements for Usui/Holy Fire® III levels I, II and ART. Also explain how to give Experiences and Ignitions.
    h. Demonstrate and practice chanting and toning.

6. Minimum class time requirements:
   The Holy Fire® III Karuna Reiki® Master class is required to be taught in a minimum of 3 days. However, you can devote more time to the class if you choose.

7. Require that a student is a Reiki master before taking any level of Karuna Reiki®. This is to ensure that the student has the use of the Usui master symbol and the ability to give attunements/Placements/Ignitions before going on to take any of the Karuna Reiki® classes.

8. Require that a student practice as a Reiki master for a minimum of 6 months before taking any level of Holy Fire® III Karuna Reiki®. This is necessary so that the student's energy field will have been conditioned to more fully accept the higher frequency energies of Holy Fire® III Karuna Reiki®

9. Conduct a written test on the symbols.

The Promise of a Thriving Reiki Practice

People come to you with many different problems, difficulties and illnesses, sometimes as a last resort, and you watch them leave relaxed, often radiant with joy and new hope...seeing them improve over time, watching them grow, gain confidence and become more trusting of life...seeing some make major changes and life adjustments...occasionally witnessing miracles...feeling the wonder of God's love pass through you and into another...sensing the presence of spiritual beings, feeling their touch, and knowing they work with you...being raised into ever greater levels of joy and peace by simply placing your hands on another...watching your life grow and develop as your continual immersion in Reiki transforms your attitudes, values and beliefs...sensing that because of your commitment to help others, beings of light are focusing their love and healing on you and carefully guiding you on your spiritual path. All this is the promise of a thriving Reiki practice!

Create a Thriving Reiki Practice, Part I
Vision, Intention and Attitudes

This article first appeared in *Reiki News Magazine* (Winter 2006).

If you've taken a Reiki class, even if it is Level I, it's possible to use your skill as a healer to start a Reiki practice. That's right; you don't need to wait until you've become a Reiki Master to start a practice. Back in the 80s, when Reiki II cost $500 and only a select few could become Reiki Masters, it was considered normal and appropriate to start an active Reiki practice after taking the first class. Keep in mind that Takata Sensei worked in Dr. Hayashi's clinic giving professional Reiki sessions to his clients with only Reiki I training.

Remember, you're not the one doing the healing; it's the Reiki energy. Its supply is unlimited, and it is guided by the highest Divine wisdom. How could you doubt that it wouldn't work right or provide the healing your clients need? One of the most important lessons the beginning Reiki practitioner or practitioners at any level can learn is to have confidence in the Reiki energy to guide you in creating the healing experience that is exactly right for each client. When you are able to set your ego aside and trust that Reiki will work, you are ready to become a Reiki practitioner. And this can be done even after taking a beginning class! In saying this, I'm talking about someone who has taken a well-organized class from a competent instructor and has also taken the time to practice by giving complete sessions with friends and family. If you've taken one of the higher degrees, that is even better, but the important thing is that if you have any level of training, as long as it was good training, you're ready to start right now.

There is tremendous value in having a thriving Reiki practice. Think about what this would look and feel like. If you had 10 clients a week and charged $75 each, you'd be earning close to $40,000 a year just from sessions. You'd likely be working 10–15 hours a week giving the sessions and an additional 10 or so hours for marketing, bookkeeping and other business activities for a total of about 25 hours a week! You'd even be able to work from your home if you wanted to. How

In the development of a thriving Reiki practice, issues, problems and challenges are bound to arise. When this happens, always remember to call on Reiki to guide you through them. There will likely be something within yourself needing to heal.

do those numbers sound? If you decided to teach, which wouldn't be difficult with that kind of clientele as potential students, you could add an additional $20,000 or more to your income. As you can see, a Reiki practice can be a real job that earns real income. There is also a special satisfaction that comes from being your own boss and running your own business.

In addition to these purely financial results, there are also emotional and spiritual benefits that can be even more fulfilling. You'll be immersed in Reiki energy several hours a day on a regular basis. This will have a positive affect on your health. At the same time, giving Reiki sessions to others and seeing them heal and grow will fill your heart with peace and joy. You'll be providing a service to others and to your community that will connect you to them in a very loving and spiritual way. Being in this type of energetic environment will quicken your personal growth and move you more quickly along on your spiritual path.

As you can see, a successful Reiki practice can provide you with both material and spiritual benefits in a way that is entirely healthy for you and your clients. Getting a successful practice started will require a clear commitment and focused activity over a period of time. Starting out with a part-time effort and eventually working at it full time, it might take six months or more of promoting and developing your practice before you begin to approach the numbers mentioned above, but a thriving Reiki practice provides rewards that are more than worth the effort it takes to create success. Think about how valuable a successful practice will be for you, your life and for those who come to see you for sessions.

The first step toward realizing your goal is to do an assessment of your inner attitudes and beliefs as well as the personal resources you possess that can be employed in the attainment of your goal.

The foundation of all we do is our inner state. It is out of this state that we are able to create what we attempt to do. Having a strong enthusiastic intention to achieve your goal is necessary. If you have a half-hearted desire or are not really excited about creating a thriving Reiki practice, or if you don't really believe you can do it, or if you feel that you don't really deserve it, then you're not likely to do very well. It takes strong motivation backed by emotional energy to achieve a goal as important as this. If you don't have this state spontaneously, or if you find yourself in a slump once you've started your project, there is something you can do to pump yourself back up. Here's an exercise that is important to do right from the beginning and continue every day. It will give you the energy and enthusiasm you need to accomplish your goal.

Goal Manifesting Exercise

1. Write your goal on a 3x5 card something like this: "I have a thriving Reiki practice. I see ten or more clients a week and teach classes. I have a thriving Reiki practice. I see ten or more clients a week and teach classes. I have a thriving Reiki practice. I see ten or more clients a week and teach classes." Be sure to repeat it three times.

2. Then place the card in your hand. If you've taken Reiki II or higher, draw all your Reiki symbols in the air over the card. If not, then simply use Reiki by itself.

3. Place the card between your hands and give it Reiki, intending that the Reiki energy empower and manifest your goal.

4. As you do this, repeat the affirmation to yourself over and over as you send it Reiki.

5. In addition, visualize yourself with a thriving Reiki practice. Picture this imagery in a field of Reiki light up above your head. See yourself looking at your client file and seeing it full of client records. See checks and money flowing into your pocket and your bank account. See yourself

in your session room working with a client knowing many more are on the way. When you visualize this, know in your heart that when this happens, it will be a truly exciting and satisfying accomplishment. Fill yourself with feelings of excitement, joy and success as though it's actually happening right now! Allow yourself to get caught up in this inner state so that you lose awareness of your surroundings and are as fully absorbed as possible in the positive feelings of having a thriving Reiki practice.

6. Do this exercise at least once a day, but more often if possible. The more you do it, the better you'll be able to enter the desired state and the more beneficial it will be for you.

This exercise is very important to practice everyday. It is part of the training you need to strengthen your energy field and cultivate the inner qualities necessary to excel at accomplishing your purpose. It is better if you do it at the same time each day, such as in the morning before you start your day or at lunchtime. Not only will it give you the personal energy to accomplish your goal and motivate you to do what you need to do, it will enhance your creativity and create a powerful magnetic force that will attract to you all the people and resources you need. This will make it much easier to develop a thriving Reiki practice.

Because Reiki energy is the basis of this process, you'll be developing a special connection to the highest level of guidance and healing. This connection will develop over time to be a wonderful source of strength, inspiration and encouragement that will help you develop all the personal qualities necessary to accomplish and even surpass your goals.

Business Consciousness
Since Reiki is a spiritual practice, some of you may have a feeling, either consciously acknowledged or lurking around in the subconscious, that spiritual things and the material world don't belong together. If this feeling is present, it needs to be dealt with and healed. There is nothing wrong with the spiritual and material working together. In fact, that's the whole purpose for spiritual beings (you and me) to be in material bodies—to bring the values and energy of the spiritual world into the material world. Having a spiritual business is an excellent way to accomplish this purpose.

Often a person may be a great healer but does not do well because he or she hasn't taken the time to develop the necessary business skills. In fact some practitioners actually shun the business aspect and then complain that they aren't making any money. This doesn't make sense. Remember, if you charge money for what you do and what you do is helping others, the better your business operates, the more people you'll be able to help, and this will directly affect your income. So don't shy away from the fact that you charge money and that you are a business person. You need to fully embrace it and be the best business person you can be.

Remember, regardless of your current knowledge or skill level, you can always improve. So even if you don't think you have the aptitude, it's important to take the time to learn and get the business aspect of your operation set up as well as you can. Some basic things you'll need are a set of books to record income and expenses and a marketing program. I'll discuss more about this in Part II of this article.

In setting up and operating your Reiki business, it's important to keep the spiritual and material in balance and working together in harmony. In your business practices, always make sure you are honest and fair in all you do and that your primary motivation is to sincerely help your clients. As your income goes up, you'll be able to expand your program and provide more services, thus helping even more people.

Money Issues

Since you're charging money for Reiki sessions and classes, your relationship to money will have a lot to do with how successful you become. Our culture seems to have a love-hate relationship with money. Remember, money is not good or bad in itself. It's no different than any other tool you might have. Think of a match. A match can be used to light a fire to cook your food or to burn down a house. Money is the same way. It's not what money is that counts, but what you do with it. If you earn your money honestly by providing services that people value and if you save and spend it wisely, then you'll be using money in a healthy way that is in alignment with the energy and principles of Reiki.

Since money is a major issue for most people, it's important for you to look at how you feel about money and heal any issues that come up. Here are some thought experiments. Try them out. You may not get negative feelings from these exercises, but if you do, it's important to think about and heal them by including the issues in your regular self-healing sessions.

Money Thought Experiment

1. How do you feel when you find out someone else might be making more money than you?
2. How do you feel when you realize that you're making more money than someone else?
3. Think about how much money you're making right now. Then think what it would be like to make twice as much or three times as much. Do you feel like you are balancing on the top of a pole, afraid you're going to fall off? Are you afraid some one is going to take your money from you or that it will be difficult to hang onto?

If you want to have a successful Reiki business, it's important for you to be connected to money in a healthy way that empowers you to establish your spiritual values in the material world. If the above thought exercises bring up unhealthy feelings, or if other experiences with money cause unhealthy feelings, it's important that you acknowledge them and heal them. Doing this will create the necessary foundation for you to live a healthy and prosperous life.

Competition

An issue that is likely to come up in your Reiki practice is competition from other Reiki practitioners. Your understanding and your attitude toward competition will play an important role in how you deal with it and how it affects your Reiki practice. Fear of competition has caused more problems and restrictions for Reiki practitioners than any other issue. This fear is based on the illusion that there isn't enough for everyone, that another Reiki teacher will take your clients or students or that if there are too many Reiki practitioners in your area, then you'll have fewer clients. Remember, FEAR is really False Evidence Appearing Real. This is especially true for Reiki. It is the fear of competition that causes problems, not competition itself.

It's important to always maintain a healthy, positive attitude toward other Reiki practitioners and teachers. If you fear them or are jealous of them or have other negative feelings toward them, then your vibration will be lowered and this will cause you to attract fewer clients. Fear of competition tends to be self-fulfilling.

There is an important lesson about this topic we can learn from Reiki. Reiki energy comes from an unlimited supply. Because of this, we'll never run out of Reiki energy, no matter how many people are giving Reiki sessions. The reason Reiki is unlimited is that it comes from a higher level of consciousness. As long as we come from a higher level of consciousness when we plan and carry out our business activities, we'll be able to tap into this same unlimited supply, which will result in abundance and prosperity in our lives.

Remember, potential Reiki clients and students are sensitive to energy. They also know that Reiki is a spiritual practice. They are looking for a practitioner/teacher who has a high vibration and who lives by spiritual values. If you have negative feelings toward other Reiki practitioners, potential customers will easily detect your attitude, and they'll tend not to be attracted to you. This will also happen subconsciously, as those interested in Reiki usually have a higher intuitive sense and will be guided away from those with a lower vibration. Therefore, it's important for you to deal with any negative feelings that come up within you and heal them. Always say positive things about other Reiki people or say nothing at all.

Reiki is guided by the highest spiritual wisdom, and it also works in other ways by guiding clients and students to the right teacher. Those who are on spiritual paths or who are seeking healing often receive help from spirit guides who are on the lookout for the right Reiki practitioners for them. Therefore it's important to maintain a high spiritual vibration and to have the attitude that no one can take students or clients away from you, and you're not taking them from other Reiki practitioners, but that all students and clients are guided to the teacher or practitioner that is right for them. This will keep you in alignment with the Reiki energy and with the highest spiritual forces that are guiding the healing community.

It's also important that the primary motivation for your Reiki practice be to truly help your clients and students. If you are overly focused on money or have a need to control others, prospective clients/students will notice this, and they will not be attracted to you. Their spirit guides will recognize this attitude even more readily and will be less likely to guide them to you. Because of this, it's really important to be clear about your motivation. A good question to ask yourself is why you want to have a thriving Reiki business. While there may be a number of good reasons, the primary one that will really work is that you truly want to help people.

Some Reiki teachers have attempted to get their students to sign noncompetitive agreements indicating that they won't teach in their territory. Others have declared that a certain area is their territory and that other teachers can't practice there. Again, this tactic is based on fear and ends up having the opposite affect than what was intended. The teacher usually ends up with less business because the energy of fear and control repels potential students and clients. Also, it's important to think in terms of how Reiki might think of a situation like this. If Reiki is focused on providing benefit to the client or student, wouldn't it be better if clients and students had more choices for potential teachers and practitioners? If you're in a situation where you're being told that you're in someone else's territory, send Reiki to the situation and follow the guidance you receive. Make sure that you respond in a way that maintains your high vibrational state and honors the values of Reiki. Remember, unless some prior agreement has been made, there are no territories in the Reiki world.

It's been found that when Reiki teachers and practitioners work together to promote Reiki, rather then competing with each other, they create a vortex of positive energy that is a much stronger attractive force than each of them working separately. This was demonstrated by Laurelle Shanti Gaia and Kathie Lipinski while they were practicing Reiki in Louisville, Kentucky. (See "Creating Harmony in the Reiki Community" in the Reiki Articles section at www.reiki.org) They organized teachers in their area who were competing with each other in negative ways and got them to work together in harmony. This may seem like a daunting task, but they called on Reiki to help and had the courage to follow their guidance. It worked! Because their group, called *United In Healing*, had so many members, they were able to organize events they wouldn't have been able to create on their own. They networked with support groups for breast cancer, fibromyalgia, diabetes and other chronic illnesses. They sponsored Reiki marathons for critically and chronically ill people and had a free clinic. In one weekend, their members had over 102 students in Reiki classes. This was a real blessing to the teachers and especially to the students and the community.

If you maintain a positive mental attitude toward members of the Reiki community in your area, your connection to Reiki will remain strong, which will allow the wisdom of Reiki to continue guiding you. This will make it easy to meditate with Reiki requesting insight on how to manage your business and how to improve it so as to attract more business, so that rather than competing, you can focus on creating. Remember, the purpose of Reiki and of your Reiki business is to provide benefit to your clients and students. If you're not getting the results you'd like, then place your focus on creating greater benefits for your clients and students. Develop your Reiki practice by taking more training to enhance your healing abilities, improving your teaching skills and the way your classes are organized, revising and upgrading your class manuals, promotional brochures, and website, or develop new teaching aids and marketing ideas. This is the positive way to deal with competition: improve your business.

In the development of a thriving Reiki practice, issues, problems and challenges are bound to arise. When this happens, always remember to call on Reiki to guide you through them. There will likely be something within yourself needing to heal. As you heal and release your inner issues, the outer issues will be resolved as well. This is the miracle of Reiki. As you focus on helping others you also benefit. And as this process unfolds, your Reiki business can turn into an important part of your spiritual path.

Part II will focus on practical ways to develop and market your Reiki practice. Before reading part II of this article I suggest you read this article again and practice the Goal Manifesting Exercise and the Money Thought Experiment along with really using the ideas in this article and giving yourself Reiki for any issues that come up. By doing so you'll have strengthened your foundation and be ready for the practical application that I'll be sharing with you in part II.

Create a Thriving Reiki Practice, Part II
This article first appeared in *Reiki News Magazine* (Spring 2007).

Part I of this article (Winter 2006) focused on developing your state of mind. This is the most important part of creating a thriving Reiki practice because everything you create originates in your mind. The quality of the thoughts and feelings that surround your goals determines your likelihood of achieving them. The clearer you create your images of success and the stronger you believe in them, the more directly you'll be manifesting your goals with your mind. To say it another way: the mind is like a broadcasting station, sending out a signal that tells the Universe what to create for you. If you believe that creating a Reiki practice will be hard and that you're not likely to get many clients, this is what the Universe will create for you. On the

techniques and methods presented here have been tested and proven to work. But you must understand that each person and each situation is different and may require a unique combination of these methods or the development of methods not mentioned here.

Here is a formula for success. If followed carefully, it will guide you to the achievement of your goals.

1. Clearly decide on your goal. This must be stated in a concrete way using numbers and dates. As an example, you might decide your goal is to average 10 Reiki clients per week within four months.

The Secret of Success

I began saying a prayer right after I received my Reiki I training. I said this prayer sincerely everyday. It guided me to be a Reiki master and inspired me to develop my Reiki practice. It has continually created miraculous results in my life. The prayer is:
Guide me and heal me so that I might be of greater service to others.

other hand, if you believe that creating a thriving Reiki practice will be easy and that you're going to have an abundant number of clients, then this is what the Universe will create for you. This is the inner marketing aspect of your business, and *it must come first*. Only by believing in yourself and the worthiness of your goals will you be able to convince others to do the same. So, if you haven't read Part I, I suggest you read it and put into practice the exercises it contains.

Assuming you are developing your inner marketing program, you can now start your outer marketing program. The ideas,

2. Develop a plan and follow it. Remember – those that fail to plan, plan to fail. Base your plan on methods others have used to achieve similar goals. The methods mentioned in this article are a good place to start. Remember to meditate with Reiki energy when contemplating the use of a particular method and in developing your plans. Reiki will guide you in miraculous ways and open doors you didn't know were there.

3. As you implement your plan, keep a record of the results you get. Note what methods work best to move

you toward your goal. Also note which ones don't work or produce poor results. It is important not to guess; keep records and look at the numbers.
4. Keep doing the things that work. Stop doing the things that don't work.
5. By eliminating the things that don't work, you'll have additional time and resources. Use them to try new things.

This may appear to be a very simple formula—because it is. Achieving success isn't a complicated process. It's just a matter of doing the right things consistently until you reach your goal. Note that even though it's a simple formula, each step is important and must be followed. As you follow this plan, over time you will develop a powerful set of business practices that move you toward your goal quickly and efficiently.

Reiki Room
You'll need a place to give your Reiki sessions. You can use a room in your home or rent an office. An office gives a more professional appearance and is a demonstration of your commitment. It is an additional business expense, but it can be cost effective by attracting more clients. However, if you can't afford it at the beginning or if you're guided to do so, it's also possible to set up a room in your home to give sessions.

You will need a Reiki table, a CD player, a couple of chairs, a table and a small filing cabinet for your records. Soft lighting, candles and incense are often helpful to create ambiance. The more relaxing and comfortable your Reiki room is, the more receptive your clients will be to the healing work you do.

Liability Insurance
I've never heard of anyone being sued for a bad Reiki session, but liability insurance can still be a good idea in some situations. Professional liability insurance will protect you if for some reason the client claims he or she was harmed by the Reiki session. The insurance company will legally represent you and negotiate with the client or defend you in court if necessary (even though this is unlikely to happen). However, the main reason to have it is that it is required by hospitals and medical clients if you should get the opportunity to give Reiki sessions there. While you usually won't receive pay for volunteering in a hospital or medical clinic, you will gain quality experience that will strengthen your professional credibility, enhance your bio, and likely increase the number of clients you have in your regular Reiki practice. It is also tremendously rewarding on an emotional and spiritual level.

General liability insurance is different from Professional liability insurance and is important for you to have. It will protect you if your client should fall off your Reiki table or if he or she slips and falls in your home or on the driveway in front of your home or in some other way becomes injured while on your property.

The Reiki Membership Association offers an excellent Reiki insurance program that includes both Professional and General liability for multiple modalities at an excellent price. Find out more at: http://www.reikimembership.com/Insurance.aspx.

Records
There are various records you'll need to keep. These include:

1. Client records: I suggest using the Client Information Form that you can download free from our Website: http://www.reiki.org/Download/FreeDownloads.html. This form informs the client that Reiki does not take the place of medical treatment. It is also a way to keep track of client contact information, as well as keeping a session history so you can check progress and see what techniques you have used and their results. It is also a way to collect email addresses for your email list, which is an important way to market your business.
2. Bookkeeping records: This can start out simply with a record book to keep track of expenses and income. You will also need a file for keeping expense receipts. You will need these for tax purposes, but it is also important to keep records to track the performance of your business and check your progress toward your goal.

Business Expenses are Tax Deductible

Because you are operating a business, you will be able to deduct business expenses from your income taxes, for which you will need records. Office rent, training expenses, including travel and lodging, as well as electricity, heat, gas for your car, and so forth may all be deducted from your taxes.

As your business expands, you may find it easier to use a computer accounting program. There are several that are free, such as Microsoft Accounting Express 2007, and others, such as Intuit or QuickBooks, that charge a fee. Besides making your bookkeeping easier, they usually include other helpful features such as a contact manager that will allow you to create a list of all your clients and contact people and which usually includes an email list manager.

Marketing Tools

You need to promote your business by letting people know who you are and the services you offer. There are many ways to do this, and it is important to try as many as possible and track the results you get from each, so you can keep doing what works and stop doing what doesn't.

It is possible to start your Reiki business on a shoestring, and this may be the best way for many to get started, but at some point, it will be necessary to increase the amount of money you spend on marketing and promotion. This can be done gradually. As you get more clients, your income will grow, and it will be possible to expand your marketing program proportionally. When spending more on promotion, it's important to carefully track your results so you can keep doing the things that are cost effective and stop doing those that aren't. At the same time, it's important to keep in mind that there are many ways to promote your business that don't involve a lot of expense.

Email List

One of the most effective things you can do to promote your Reiki practice is develop an email list of those interested in Reiki. In today's world people use email to communicate far more than snail mail. This is because email is easy, fast and inexpensive. If you're promoting your Reiki practice, it's easier to compose an email and send it to your email list than to mail a flyer. With email, it's as easy as clicking a mouse button a few times, and it's done with almost no expense. With snail mail, it will take hours or days to get the mailing ready, and the expense can be in the hundreds or even thousands of dollars. Email is the way to go and results are almost instantaneous.

Because of this, it's important to begin collecting email addresses of those interested in Reiki right away. Collect them from your clients by having them fill in their email addresses on your Client Information Form and collect them from all the promotions and events you're involved with.

You can use your email list to remind people about your Reiki practice, let them know about promotions or special deals you have, or about your Free Reiki Evenings or Fund Raisers and so forth. *An effective email list is the most important marketing tool you can develop.*

Many email software programs allow you to send to a large list without the whole email list going to each recipient. There are bulk email websites that provide online software for sending out to large lists, and you can also get your own software programs and install them on your computer or on your Web server. Do a Google search for Bulk Email Service to locate providers. One email program I recommend is Subscribe Me Pro http://www.siteinteractive.com/subpro/ This program is only $59.00 and provides tracking.

To learn more about the importance of email for marketing I suggest you go to the Guerrilla Marketing website at www.gmarketing.com and read their article on email and marketing. You will also find other interesting articles there. I recommend you order the book, Mastering Guerrilla Marketing, which explains how to achieve your marketing goals with minimum expense.

Web Site

While a website isn't a necessity and you can start your Reiki practice without one, it's important to get a website as soon as possible to take advantage of its important marketing features. A website is a handy way to let people know what you do. Rather than trying to give a detailed verbal description of your services to people, or give them a bunch of handouts, just give them your web address. They will have access to all of your material and be able to read through it at their leisure and return again and again until they convince themselves to come to you for a session. Also, the Web is such an integral part of society now that if you don't have a website, most people will think you're not serious about your business.

A well-designed Reiki website needs to contain:

1. An explanation of Reiki, including a Frequently Asked Questions section.
2. A description of your sessions, how long they last, your fee, etc. Testimonials from your clients are also a big plus.
3. If you're teaching, include a class schedule and a complete description of what each class contains, and what students will be able to do after taking each class. Class fees and prerequisites should also be listed.
4. A bio of yourself including a picture and especially your training background and experience.
5. Articles you have written about Reiki.
6. An email collection box to collect email addresses of visitors to your site.
7. Contact information including phone, email address, city and state, but not

your home or business street address. Your exact location, including a map, can be sent separately to those who have scheduled a session or signed up for a class. This will prevent people from coming by without an appointment.

You can start out with a simple site that you design, but after a while, it's a good idea to have a professional webmaster design and set up your website. Remember that people will determine who you are by the quality of the promotional material you provide. So make sure your website looks professional, is well organized, clearly communicates your ideas and provides useful information. One way to find a good webmaster is to find websites online that you like and contact the webmasters of those sites to find out how much they charge for web design, and get a feel for whether you can work with them, etc.

As I mentioned above, an important feature for your website is an email collection box. This provides a method for you to collect the email addresses of those who frequent your website. Subscribe Me Pro provides a method of setting this up. To get people to give you their email address, you'll need to offer them something. You could offer to give them a podcast or recording of a Reiki talk or meditation you've recorded or to receive a free Reiki newsletter or something of that nature. Be sure to place a value on what they'll get such as $5 or $10.

Business Cards
It's important to have a business card listing your name, phone and, especially, your email address and website, along with your business name, if you have one, and the Reiki services you offer. It's better not to list your street address to prevent people from coming to your office without an appointment. A business card lets people know you're serious and professional and makes it easy for people to contact you. Carry them with you at all times. You will be surprised at the number of opportunities to pass out your cards, especially when you're focused on the promotion of your Reiki practice.

Short Explanation of Reiki
Create short, succinct answers for basic Reiki questions so you'll be ready to explain Reiki to those who express interest. When people ask what Reiki is, I usually say; *"Reiki is a Japanese technique for relaxation that also promotes healing. It's done through touch. A warm and soothing energy flows from the hands into the client, promoting relaxation and releasing tension."* This answer usually inspires comments such as: "I could really use something like that." Or "Boy do we really need that around here." If you get a positive response like this, offer to give a short demo of five minutes or so to treat the person's shoulders or anywhere they may have tension or an ache or pain. Then give them a business card and answer any other questions they may have. They may contact you for a session or may refer others.

Impromptu Reiki Sessions
When you're out and about, talk to people, and weave the fact that you do Reiki into your conversation. If they ask what Reiki is, give them the short explanation above and offer to give them a short demo. Just place your hands on their shoulders to show them how the energy feels. Often they'll say things like, "I really need this," or "Wow that's going right for my sore arm," or "My headache is going away." Or you may be

talking to someone and they mention an ache or pain they have. Immediately offer to give them Reiki for it. Many times, they'll already know what Reiki is, or if not, then give them your short explanation. Then let them know you do professional Reiki sessions and give them your card. You could also go on to explain how Reiki can help those undergoing chemotherapy and how it promotes healing after surgery and so forth. A hands-on experience like this will leave an impression, and even if they don't sign up for a session, they may refer others to you. Most will know of someone going into the hospital or in need of healing for one condition or another.

This technique is great at parties. You can either weave into your conversations that you do Reiki or those you talk with may offer that they have an ache or pain or a tense situation at work, which is a great lead-in for offering them Reiki. Once you start giving a demo session, often a crowd will gather, and you can give a little talk about Reiki to those watching as you give the session. Afterwards, pass out your business cards to those interested.

Upward Price Technique
If you are just starting a Reiki practice, try this technique for motivating people to come to you for sessions. When someone asks how much you charge, say, "I'm giving 10 sessions for free, and I've already given four (or whatever the number is at that point). Then say, "After the 10 free sessions, I'm going to be charging $10.00 per session." This will motivate people to sign up right away so they get a free session and avoid having to pay $10.00. After you've given out your 10 free sessions when someone asks how much you charge, say, "I'm giving 10 sessions for $10 each, and I've already given three (or whatever the number is at that point). After the 10, my price is going up to $20 per session." This will continue to motivate people to get sessions from you while the price is low. Continue with this process until you reach your target fee. By working like this, you'll be charging a fee based on your experience, and you will be motivating people to come to you quickly for sessions so they will save money.

Target Fee
Your target fee is the fee you want to work up to for Reiki sessions after you've gained experience, developed your business and have a steady stream of clients. Your target fee will vary depending on the part of the country you live in. Doing a little research will help you figure this out. One way is to check with other experienced Reiki practitioners in your area to see what they charge. Another way is to set your target fee in the same range as professional massage therapists are charging in your area. Also remember that additional factors to consider when determining your target fee are the amount of training you've had, the amount of experience and the results clients get from your sessions.

Clients Are Your Best Promoters
Those who have experienced your work are the best people to promote you. Make sure you give every client some of your business cards to hand out to friends, family and acquaintances who could use Reiki sessions.

Bonus Program
Creating a bonus program based on clients getting free sessions for bringing you new paying clients is also a way to promote your practice. When you give your clients

business cards to pass out, tell them that for every two paying clients they send to you, you'll give them a free session. When clients come to you, you'll need to ask them how they found out about your practice and if anyone referred them to you. Use an Excel spreadsheet to keep track of how many each client referred to you. When a client gets the required number, email them and let them know they've earned a free session. Concerning the number they need to get a free session, remember that the idea is to build up your Reiki practice quickly and that each new client could become a promoter of your business too. Keeping the required number low will motivate them to work harder promoting your business.

Professional Referrals
Make friends with the chiropractors, massage therapists, acupuncturists, aroma therapists, medical doctors and other professionals in your area and let them know that you'll refer clients to them, if they'll refer clients to you. Collect business cards from them and give each some of yours. If they are hesitant to do this, offer them a free session, and then give them some of your cards to give to their clients. This method can also open the possibility of being offered a job giving sessions at a clinic.

Flyers
It's good to have a basic flyer to promote your business. Carry them with you to place on bulletin boards in health food stores, bookstores, churches, and so forth and to give to prospective clients. Include a brief explanation of Reiki and the benefits it provides. If possible, include testimonials from your clients. Also be sure to create special flyers to reflect new promotions or services you're offering.

Magazine Advertising
I would be leaving out an important marketing method if I failed to mention advertising in the *Reiki News Magazine*. The magazine goes directly to 20,000 people who have a serious interest in Reiki, and it's a fact that those who advertise in our magazine get results. This is especially true for those who provide professional advertising copy and graphics and advertise regularly. If you want to find the ads that are working, check the current issue and then work your way through previous issues to see who's advertising consistently. The ads that appear in multiple issues are the ones that are working because people don't continue advertising unless it is cost effective.

Free Reiki Evening
This is also called a Reiki Share group and is an evening usually offered on a regular basis, such as once or twice a month, when Reiki practitioners get together to exchange Reiki. People who have never experienced Reiki can also be invited. Those who have Reiki training are asked to bring their Reiki tables. Usually a talk is given at the beginning that explains Reiki and answers questions. Usually, those new to Reiki receive sessions first, often with several practitioners giving them Reiki at the same time. A table can be set up for practitioners to display their business cards and flyers. Announcements about classes or other Reiki activities can also be made. Include a registration sheet to get names and email addresses to add to your email list so you can keep them notified about future Reiki events.

This is an excellent way to meet new Reiki practitioners, attract those seeking healing and to advertise your practice.

A subtle benefit of these meetings is that it keeps Reiki awareness high in your community and creates good will that will come back to you to support your practice. See "How to Create a Successful Reiki Share" in the summer 2014 issue of *Reiki News Magazine*.

Fundraisers
Non-profit organizations such as churches and charity groups often sponsor fundraising events. You could volunteer to set up and operate a Reiki fundraising event to benefit a group you wish to support. In this event, you provide free Reiki sessions and the clients give either a donation or a fixed fee to the organization. Be sure to create a sign-up sheet that includes the recipient's email address so you can add them to your email list. Explain on the sign-up sheet that you may use their email address to let them know about other Reiki events. Operating a Reiki fundraiser will give you valuable experience and enhance your professional reputation. You will also have the satisfaction of helping a group you believe in at the same time you're helping those who receive your Reiki sessions. Once the event is over, you're likely to get people wanting to come to you for additional Reiki sessions. See The Saga of a Reiki Fundraiser on page 32 of the Spring 2007 issue of *Reiki News Magazine* for more information.

Holistic Fairs
Getting a booth at a holistic fair can be another effective way to promote your Reiki practice. Get several Reiki practitioners to help you. Take a Reiki table, a sign and plenty of business cards and flyers. Offer ten or fifteen- minute Reiki sessions for $10 and have three or more Reiki practitioners giving the sessions to each person. Create a sign-up sheet that includes the recipient's email address. It's possible to generate income at the same time you promote your Reiki business.

These are a few of the many ways you can promote your Reiki business. As you try these ideas, and especially if you follow the manifesting meditation practice in Part I of this series, you'll come up with additional ways that are just right for you. As you move forward and achieve your goal, you'll experience the miracle-working power of Reiki manifesting abundance in your life. Usui Sensei said, "Reiki is the secret art of inviting happiness." Certainly you will experience a great happiness as you create a thriving Reiki practice. May you always be blessed by the radiant light of Reiki.

May the followers of all religions and spiritual paths work together to create peace among all people on earth

World Peace

*May the followers of all religions and
spiritual paths work together to create
peace among all people on Earth.*
—INSCRIPTION ON THE WORLD PEACE CRYSTAL GRID

This article first appeared in *Reiki News Magazine* (Winter 2004).

Introduction

I conceived the idea for the World Peace Crystal Grid in 1997 as a way for Reiki people and others to create world peace. The Grid is made with copper and quartz crystals, materials that allow it to collect healing energy and send it into the world to promote peace. The philosophy embodied in its inscription is based on the idea that peace will come to the world quickly once the world's religions and spiritual people honor each other and work together in harmony to promote world peace. Peace Grids have been placed at the North and South Poles and recently in Jerusalem.

World Peace Is Possible

There is tremendous value within the teachings of the religious and spiritual organizations of the world and these teachings have had a very positive affect on the well-being of humanity. At the same time the resources of religion have sometimes been redirected to produce results that have not expressed their highest principles. In fact some feel that religion has been the cause of at least some of the war and suffering in the world. This is unfortunate because this is not the purpose of religion.

Religious intolerance seems to be the cause of most of this difficulty, and this is unnecessary. The core values of most religions and spiritual paths are very similar and represent a common purpose that could be used to unite them to work together for worthy goals.

In fact these core values are important spiritual principles that have the power to solve our problems and bring peace to the Earth. The following are a few of these principles:

Free Will

Free will is a God-given right that is a primary tenet of most religions. Because of this principle, everyone has the right to decide for him or herself which religion to follow—or to follow none at all. To fully honor this principle is to honor other religions and spiritual paths and the choice others have made to follow them.

Forgiveness

Letting go of hate and the desire for revenge is healthy not only for those forgiven, but especially for the forgiver. This is the healthy way to move forward and solve problems between groups, whereas revenge only perpetuates war and suffering for everyone.

Love

This is the greatest principle of all, as love is the greatest power. It is important that the value of love be fully understood and acted on as it is through love that our highest and most valued qualities are strengthened and expressed. There is no limit to the extent that the power of love can be developed, and it is this principle above all others that is capable of creating peace between all people on Earth.

There is tremendous power within all religions and spiritual paths, and if each would work from its highest values, accept each other and work together in harmony, it would be easy for them to create world peace. So powerful would this force be that all the problems of the world could be easily and quickly solved! By working together with trust and respect, rather than opposing each other, each will be able to practice its religious principles in peace and will more easily be able to ensure the health and well-being of its members.

The Peace Grid Is Conceived

When I lived in Hawaii, I started to write a novel about someone who had discovered a plan to save the Earth. The plan had been developed during Atlantean times by a group of white magicians. Their plan involved storing a set of twelve crystals to await the right time to place them at the North Pole, where they would be activated by cosmic energies to heal the Earth and bring peace. The crystals had been hidden in various locations around the world—caves, museums, isolated native societies, etc. The main character's job was to travel around gathering the crystals and then take them to the North Pole, where they would be activated.

I never finished the novel, but after moving back to the Detroit area, I heard of an artist who had traveled to the North Pole to meditate. When I heard what he had done, it inspired me to do something similar. I began planning my trip, and after finding a way to get to the North Pole, began to consider what I would do once there. I thought about the ideas from the novel and realized that I would be able to do something similar to what the main character had done. This is when the idea of the Peace Grid came into being. I worked with Steve Burr, an artist who had created other Reiki jewelry for me, to design the Peace Grid.

How the Grid Works

The Grid was designed to act like a battery that can be charged with Reiki energy, which it then sends out to the Earth to create peace. The Peace Grids at the North and South Poles make use of the Earth's magnetic field, which flows through the poles. This magnetic energy is the Earth's aura, and the North and South Poles are like the Earth's crown and root chakras. With the Grids placed here, their energy is carried into the aura of the Earth to completely surround it with healing and peace. The Peace Grid in Jerusalem is in an especially strategic location as it makes use of the intense spiritual energies from the world's three main monotheistic religions, Judaism, Christianity and Islam, which have their most important shrines in Jerusalem.

A Description of the Grid

The Grid is twelve inches in diameter and made of solid copper. With twelve petals, it has the shape of the heart chakra and is plated with a layer of nickel for protection and an outer layer of 24-carat gold. There are double-terminated quartz crystals on each petal. Inside the circle of crystals is a circle of twelve symbols that represents the major religions of the world, including independent spiritual paths, native peoples and all others. These

| Native Peoples | Buddhism | Hinduism | Independent Spiritual Paths | Christianity | Judaism |

| Goddess Religions | Islam | Shintoism | All Others *including Agnostics & Athiests* | Zoroastrianism | Taoism |

Symbols on the World Peace Crystal Grid

symbols are listed below. In the center is a cone-shaped crystal with twelve facets, each facing one of the twelve symbols, crystals and petals. Under the central crystal are Reiki symbols; one is the Karuna Reiki® symbol for peace, and the other is the CKR, whose purpose is to increase the strength of the energy. The inscription reads:

May the followers of all religions and spiritual paths work together to create peace among all people on Earth.

Using the Grid to Create World Peace

After placing the Peace Grids at each location, I took photographs and have made these available to those who want to help. The idea is for those with Reiki to use the photos to send distant Reiki to the Peace Grids and charge them with healing energy. Thousands of copies of the North and South Pole pictures have been passed out, and copies of all three are at the end of this article. Copies of all the pictures can also be downloaded from our website at www.reiki.org.

Those who send Reiki to the Grids have noticed that a feeling of peace comes to them each time they do it, and those who send consistently have found that their lives become more peaceful and that they tend to function as peacemakers among the people they associate with. The Reiki that is sent to the Peace Grids charges them to fulfill their purpose, which works on many levels. The Peace Grids, guided by the Higher Power, automatically send healing energy to crisis situations on the planet, and at the same time they inspire and empower people everywhere to work toward peace.

The North Pole

This is the first location a Peace Grid was placed, May 1997. The following is a brief account of this experience:

A cold wind whipped across the gravel runway as I walked from the plane to the small airport terminal at Resolute in Canada's Northwest Territory. It had taken two days to get there after teaching a Karuna class in New York City, yet I still had over eight hours of flight time before I would get to the North Pole.

A ski and dog sled team was going to the North Pole and would be picked up by plane once they arrived. There were a few extra seats on the plane and when planning my trip, I had made arrangements to go along. I had to wait for the right weather conditions at the Pole before we could continue, but I also had to be ready to leave at a moment's notice. After several days of hanging out at the station, we were told it was time.

It took six hours to reach our first stop, and as we flew over the pristine environment with only ice, snow and the tops of mountains visible, reality intensified and I was overcome by a tremendous sense of adventure.

We stopped at Eureka weather station on Ellesmere Island to refuel but had to stay as the weather at the pole had changed. We continued on the next day, but then had to return to Eureka after only a few hours because the weather didn't hold. After another day we took off again and, landing on the Arctic ice, picked up the dog sled team.

We loaded the dog sled, the dogs and the team members onto the plane and proceeded on. The team had not made it to the Pole, so we were going to fly the remainder of the distance and land there. However, when we got over the Pole, it was covered with fog, and the pilot couldn't see the ice clearly enough to land, so we circled and came back.

I was disappointed that I hadn't placed the Peace Grid at the Pole and was not sure what to do. I made a call to the Center asking people to send Reiki energy to help the project, and then I talked to the flight dispatcher to see if I could get on another flight.

There are actually two North Poles;

From top: North Pole trip: Air terminal at Resolute. Refueling at Eureka Weather Station. We had to carry extra fuel in the plane. Sled dogs on the Arctic ice.

one is geographic and the other magnetic. I chose the geographic pole simply because I was offered a ride there. I didn't know there were flights to the magnetic pole, even though this was the best place for the Peace Grid. After Reiki had been sent, the situation changed.

The flight dispatcher became sympathetic to our cause and got me on a flight to the magnetic North Pole, which is near Ellef Ringnes Island.

After landing, I walked away from the plane on the sea ice. There I dedicated the World Peace Crystal Grid and gave it a final charge of Reiki. I took a picture for use by those wanting to send distant Reiki to it, and then buried it deep in the snow. When the sea ice melted in July, it would sink to the bottom of the Arctic Ocean where it would remain forever.

The South Pole

In December 1999, I traveled to Punta Arenas at the southern tip of Chile, my first stop on my way to the South Pole to place the second Peace Grid. I waited here until the weather cleared at our landing site at Patriot Hills in Antarctica. After four days I was notified we'd be taking off in a few hours.

After arriving at Patriot Hills, I was assigned a tent that was solar heated. The outside temperature was -30 degrees F, but because the sun is up all the time and the tents are designed to retain solar energy, the inside of the tent was much warmer—sometimes it got up to +30 degrees F.

Our special clothing and sleeping bags were warm; in fact I never felt cold, except for a small section around my wrists and near my neck. The main tent at Patriot Hills was the dining tent, which had snow melters inside to create drinking water. This kept it nice and warm, and most people hung out there while they waited for the

From top: South Pole trip: Fellow adventurers in the dining tent at Patriot Hills. DC-3 at the South Pole. At the South Pole. Charging the Grid before burying it in the snow.

weather to clear so they could fly out to their destinations. The pilots, world-class skiers, mountain climbers and explorers who were there would sit around telling stories of their previous adventures, which were fascinating.

After four days the weather cleared and we took off for the South Pole. Our plane was a modified DC3 with skis. We were scheduled to have a three-hour escorted tour of the Pole and the scientific station, and then we would have to leave. This would have been far too short for what I needed to do with the Peace Grid. So, I was resigned to placing it at Patriot Hills after I got back.

Fortunately, my luck changed with the weather. After we got to the South Pole station we were taken on the tour. As we got back to the plane, we were told that the weather at Patriot Hills had gotten worse, and we would have to stay at the Pole until conditions improved. There was no room at the science station, so we had to stay in our tents.

We spent five days there before the weather cleared at Patriot Hills and we could leave. This gave me lots of time to meditate with the Peace Grid and find an appropriate spot to place it.

Reiki Class at the South Pole

While at the South Pole I taught a mini Reiki class with two women students. This was their first camping experience, and with a wind chill of -60 degrees F and an altitude of 10,000 feet, they were very uncomfortable. So I thought I would try to cheer them up. First I offered Reiki sessions, which they gladly accepted. Then I brought them some hot water and biscuits and suggested that I could teach them Reiki. They liked this even better. I explained how Reiki works, gave them the attunement and had them practice on

From top: Entrance to the Oil Press Art Gallery - the light beam just happened to be there when I took the picture. Oil Press stones. Smudging during class inside the gallery.

each other. They loved it and were much happier. In fact, one woman said Reiki helped her keep warm, and the other said she was more relaxed and better able to cope with the difficult conditions. Also, after returning to Patriot Hills I gave a Reiki talk in the dining tent and taught another Reiki class with eight students.

The energy in Antarctica and especially at the South Pole is phenomenal! It is a very pure environment with thousands of miles of nothing but snow and ice. Only the tops of mountains called nunataks are visible, sticking up out of the glacial ice, and at that time of year, the sun is shining all the time. Being so close to the magnetic pole, and at a high altitude, there's a wonderful feeling of intensity, clarity and peace.

During my five-day stay at the South Pole, I had some wonderful meditations. I was able to sit on the exact South Pole with the Peace Grid, and at the same time, tune into the one at the North Pole, and then experience the huge ball of the Earth between the poles. I could feel tremendous energy, and I sent Reiki and prayed for peace on Earth. I was able to do this a number of times. I also did the Reiki moving meditation, asking that my divine mission on Earth be fulfilled. These were all intensely powerful, and it was during one of these experiences that I had a personal healing of great importance, which continued to unfold for several weeks. This was a major piece that I had been working with for many years, and now that it is complete, I can see that this experience was a turning point that opened new possibilities for my work as a healer and teacher.

After several days of meditation and picture taking, I performed a special ritual and buried the Peace Grid at the South Pole the day before we left. It will

From top: Doorway to the ancient wall that surrounded Solomon's Temple. There are miles of streets like this. Another street scene.

125

remain there, slowly becoming buried deeper beneath the surface as each year's snowfall accumulates.

Jerusalem

Last year I traveled to Israel to teach Reiki and began thinking about the importance a Peace Grid would have there for creating peace between Israel and Palestine and in the Middle East. I considered several locations. It needed to be a place where the Grid would remain undisturbed for an extended period of time, and the location also needed to be sacred or possess special energy. As an example, the North and South Pole locations are ideal as they are strategic, have tremendous energy and are so remote that no one will ever find them. In Israel, I considered placing the Grid at the bottom of the Sea of Galilee or the Dead Sea or burying it in the desert, but none of these locations seemed like the right one. The Sea of Galilee is shallow, and the Grid might be found and removed, the Dead Sea is so salty it could easily corrode the Grid, and the desert didn't seem to have the right energy. After visiting Old Jerusalem, I realized this would be the right location, but finding a place where it could be left undisturbed was challenging.

I wanted to return to teach in Israel again and was intent on teaching in Old Jerusalem. I asked Amir, who sponsored my first class, if he would try to find a room there for a Reiki class. He was doubtful and at first found nothing. Then I was inspired to send Reiki to the situation and also worked on the project with my clairvoyant therapist. Working this way—and with the help of my guide, Jesus—we were able to contact and gain acceptance from the regional spirits who oversee the energy around the Old City.

After gaining their blessing, Amir had

From top: With the Peace Grid at the Western Wall. Peace Grid leaning against the Western Wall. Hooded figure.

a breakthrough. He was introduced to the owner of an art gallery that was well known and influential. After talking with him and realizing that there really wasn't much other choice, Amir thought to ask him if he would allow the class to be held in his gallery. The owner liked the fact that Reiki was a healing art and that Amir was using it to help others, especially children, and so he agreed to allow us to have the class there. In addition, he agreed to provide a place for the Peace Grid within his store. This was an ideal location for both the class and the Peace Grid! The Grid could be hung on the wall for people to see, yet would be safe with all the other artwork.

The Oil Press Art Gallery is in a 1,500-year-old building, and until recently had been used to produce sesame oil using a set of giant stones that were turned by a camel. Also, the owner had started to create a hole in the wall for a safe by chipping on the soft stone with a hammer. When he came to very hard stone, he knew he had discovered something important and called in an archeologist who told him that he had uncovered part of the original 3,000-year-old wall of the city that had surrounded Solomon's Temple. Abir, the owner, has turned this into a small alcove where the wall can be seen.

Abir was very warm and welcoming and took time to make sure we had everything we needed for the class. He also arranged for us to meditate on a rooftop where many of the sacred sites within and around the city could be seen. The class was very special. The combination of Karuna Reiki® and the ancient spiritual consciousness within the Old City worked together to create an experience that was very uplifting.

Old Jerusalem is a walled city with

From top: Passageway. Dome of the Rock. Tombs of Bene Hezir and Zechariah in the Kidron Valley outside the Old City.

seven gates, and it is divided into different quarters, including the Muslim, Jewish, Christian and Armenian quarters. When you walk through the narrow, crowded streets you won't find any signs telling you when you've passed from one quarter to another, and it's not obvious; but if you're perceptive, you can tell. There are more than a hundred streets, with many side streets and narrow passageways mostly lined with small shops and vendors selling many interesting things—cloth, carpets, incense, spices, grain, vegetables, meat and fish, candles, religious objects and art of all kinds. The shops are usually only about ten feet wide and right next to each other. Many of the streets are covered; some are well lit, but others are dark.

Within this labyrinth are some of the most sacred religious sites in the world. The Stations of the Cross, which mark the route Jesus carried the cross, are here, along with Golgotha, where he was crucified and his tomb. The Jewish Western Wall, which is the only intact section from Solomon's Temple, and the Muslim Dome of the Rock, where Muhammad is said to have ascended into heaven, are also here. Priests, nuns and holy people from many countries walk the streets dressed in their traditional religious garb, along with beggars, locals, children and tourists. An air of mystery, intrigue and excitement is everywhere. The whole scene seems like it's straight out of Indiana Jones!

As you walk past the shops, the shop owners constantly call to you, inviting you into their stores. Some look you right in the eye as though you are their best friend, give you a warm smile and tell you how glad they are to see you. But as you go along, you soon find this is only a ploy to gain your confidence

From top: Church of Saint Mary Magdalene. Ancient olive trees in the Garden of Gethsemane. Abir and I in gallery with Peace Grid.

so they can sell you something. In an environment like this, it's best to remain centered in your own energy and focus on where you're going.

There are also lots of young Israeli solders carrying automatic weapons as well as private armed security guards with radios. Although their presence can initially create hesitation, they probably keep the Old City safe.

After the Reiki class, I had time to focus on the Peace Grid. Abir graciously gave me the freedom to place it anywhere in the gallery I chose. There were several places I had in mind, but as I meditated on which would be the best, I noticed interference entering my auric field. I began feeling weak and knew this was something I needed to deal with. I also realized that I had been having these uneasy feelings off and on ever since I had taken the Peace Grid to the gallery, but had been too focused on the class to pay attention to them.

As I tuned in, I could see a group of spirits who were very angry at me and didn't trust what I was doing. They didn't understand the Peace Grid and thought the symbols on it were harmful. They were priests who had seen their temple desecrated in the past and were very suspicious of outsiders bringing things to their sacred space. They thought the Grid might contain an evil spell that would cause problems for them and their religion.

On sensing this, I returned to my room, where I said some prayers asking for help from the Higher Power and also calling on my guides and angels to heal the situation. When I began sending Reiki, Jesus came and started to interact with the spirits. In a non-threatening way, he explained to them that I was not trying to harm them or their religion, but that I was working to create peace. Jesus then showed them a very powerful form of love, which seemed to open their hearts. He proceeded to show how their past opposition to other religions had only created problems for their religion and that if they could focus on love and on promoting peace between religions, they would be able to enjoy their own religion even more. He then took them up to a higher dimension where they could again be in their old temple, the one that had been destroyed by outsiders. They were very thankful for this experience and accepted the healing this brought to them. As Jesus continued to work with them, he showed them the value of forgiveness and how healthy it was for them to forgive those who had harmed them in the past. As they gave up their anger, a feeling of peace came to them, and they became more and more open to working with these higher energies.

It was apparent that a breakthrough was taking place and that these spirit priests, who were guiding the human leaders of their religion, would be making use of these new methods and helping to bring peace to their people. It seemed that this was the beginning of an important process and that they would continue to receive lessons about the power of love and the importance of peace.

This was a revelation to me as well. I was amazed by what was happening, and yet it all made sense and I was very thankful to be a part of this wonderful experience.

After this healing process had begun, I decided to take the Peace Grid to some of the sacred sites around the Old City to pray for peace and ask that the Grid be charged with the spiritual energies of each location. I first went to the Western Wall. Leaning the Peace Grid against the wall, I prayed for peace between all the religions of the world. As I did this I felt the tremendous energy of the Wall enter into the Peace Grid to empower it.

Next I went to the Church of the Holy Sepulcher. I arrived at four in the morning and was asked if I'd like to be present in the tomb while the priest gave Mass. The space was so small that only the priest, I, and two others were able to be present. After the Mass was over and the others had left, I said prayers for world peace and sent Reiki to the Grid. I did something similar at the foot of the cross at Golgotha, which is also located in the church.

Next I went to the Church of All Nations where the stone that Jesus prayed on the night before his arrest in the garden of Gethsemane is located. I prayed and did more Reiki with the Grid there.

After that I climbed the steep hill up the Mount of Olives. At the top I found the Church of the Ascension, which commemorates the spot where Jesus ascended into heaven. While waiting for the man to come with the key, I began wondering where the best place to meditate would be and as I walked in front of the church I felt as though I was becoming very light and experienced an uplifting feeling. This seemed like a good sign, so I sat on the steps and meditated with the Grid there.

A little farther down the road is a scenic lookout point giving a view of the whole city, and here I sat and meditated while focusing on the Dome of the Rock. I prayed specifically that Islam and all the religions and spiritual paths of the world would work together to create peace on Earth.

This was a very wonderful and sacred time and after this, I felt the Peace Grid was ready to be placed in the gallery. I met Abir at the gallery and he helped mount the Grid on the wall. After taking pictures I heaved a sigh of relief knowing that my work in Jerusalem had been completed.

The global Reiki community is composed of members of all religions and spiritual paths located in most of the countries on the planet. This is an ideal group of people to create world peace because together we hold the vibration of everyone on Earth! As we work together consistently using the awesome power of Reiki, we'll be creating one of the most important transformations that has ever occurred on the planet. As world peace develops, society will be lifted up to a level of well-being and happiness that will make undreamed of conditions possible. But we must take action now! The Peace Grid system has been set up to make it easy for you to send Reiki for world peace. As you send Reiki to it, your life will become more peaceful too, and you'll become part of a team of Reiki people around the world who are working for world peace. May your heart be deeply blessed as you enjoy the peace you help create.

Jerusalem Location: The Oil Press Art Gallery, 33 Jewish Quarter Road, Jerusalem, Israel 97500 email oilpress@netvision.net.il. The Peace Grid was placed here in October 2004.

If you'd like to read more about these experiences and see additional pictures, go to www.reiki.org

Reiki Symbol Quiz

Teachers Name: _____ Class Date: _____

Class Location - City: _____ State: _____

What caused you to take this Reiki Class: (please circle all that apply)

reiki.org - Internet site   Teachers - personal internet site   Open House/Reiki Share

From a Friend   Reiki News   Other _____

Please Circle Class: Reiki II   Holy Fire® III Reiki Master   Holy Fire® III Karuna Master

---

Student Name (please print) _____

Mailing Address: _____ City: _____

State: _____ Zip: _____ Country: _____

Phone number: _____ E-mail: _____

Please draw the symbols for this class level below and/or on the back without looking at your notes. Be sure to include the names of the symbols. The numbers and arrows are not necessary.

Reiki Client Information Form

Name: (Please Print) _____
Phone (home): _____ Cell phone or evening: _____
Address: _____
City, State, Zip: _____
Email (optional): _____
Emergency Contact: _____
Current Medications and dosage: _____
_____
_____

Are you currently under the care of a physician? ___ Yes ___ No
If yes, physician's name: _____
How did you hear about us? _____
_____

Have you ever had a Reiki session before? ___Yes ___No
If yes, when was your last session? _____
Number of previous sessions _____

Do you have a particular area of concern? _____
_____
_____

Are you sensitive to perfumes or fragrances? _____
Are you sensitive to touch? _____

I understand that Reiki is a simple, gentle, hands-on energy technique that is used for stress reduction and relaxation. I understand that Reiki practitioners do not diagnose conditions nor do they prescribe or perform medical treatment, prescribe substances, nor interfere with the treatment of a licensed medical professional. I understand that Reiki does not take the place of medical care. It is recommended that I see a licensed physician or licensed healthcare professional for any physical or psychological ailment I may have. I understand that Reiki can complement any medical or psychological care I may be receiving. I also understand that the body has the ability to heal itself and to do so, complete relaxation is often beneficial. I acknowledge that long term imbalances in the body sometimes require multiple sessions in order to facilitate the level of relaxation needed by the body to heal itself.

Signed: _____ Date: _____

Privacy Notice:
No information about any client will be discussed or shared with any third party without written consent of the client or parent/guardian if the client is under 18.

Reiki Documentation Form

Client Name: _____ Date: _____

Reason for Session
___ Relaxation and Stress Reduction
___ Specific Issue:
     Physical _____
     _____

     Emotional _____
     _____

     Mental/Spiritual _____
     _____

Changes since last session: _____
_____
_____

Observation / Scan before Reiki Session: _____
_____
_____
_____

Observation / Scan after Reiki Session: _____
_____
_____
_____

Post Session Notes: _____
_____
_____
_____
_____
_____
_____

Length / Type of Session: _____
Follow up Planned: _____
_____
_____

Practitioner Name: _____

Evaluation
Holy Fire® III Karuna Reiki® Master Training

Please help us gauge the effectiveness of this seminar and plan for future offerings by answering the following questions as completely as possible:

Name: _____

Mailing Address: _____

Email Address: _____

Class Location: _____ Dates (MM/DD/YYYY): _____

Instructor: _____

Attainment of Objectives:

Please rate the teacher's effectiveness in leading each activity.

Day 1:		5 - Excellent 1 - Poor
1.	Explanation of the ICRT's definition of Soul and Spirit, the Heavens and Letting Go of Guides	5 4 3 2 1
2.	Explanation of the unique way of doing Holy Fire® III Experiences, Placements and Ignitions	5 4 3 2 1
3.	Explanation of the Healing in the River of Life experience	5 4 3 2 1
4.	Healing in the River of Life experience	5 4 3 2 1
5.	Explanation of a brief history of Reiki and how Reiki has evolved with Usui, Hayashi and Takata	5 4 3 2 1
6.	Explanation of Holy Fire® concepts	5 4 3 2 1
7.	Explanation of Holy Fire® III Karuna Reiki®, including its origin	5 4 3 2 1
8.	Explanation of Holy Fire® III Reiki and spiritual guidance	5 4 3 2 1
9.	Explanation that this class is both a practitioner and master class	5 4 3 2 1
10.	Explanation that after this class, all future classes - at every level, may be taught as Holy Fire® classes	5 4 3 2 1
11.	Explanation of how Placements work, and that we now give Placements for Holy Fire® III Reiki I, II & ART	5 4 3 2 1
12.	Explanation of the Ignition Process	5 4 3 2 1

Holy Fire® and Karuna Reiki® are registered service marks of William Lee Rand

13.	First Ignition	5 4 3 2 1
14.	Explanation of the Holy Fire® symbol & energy, test	5 4 3 2 1
15.	Explanation of all of the Karuna I & II symbols, what they're used for, how to draw them, test	5 4 3 2 1

Day 2:		5 – Excellent 1 - Poor
1.	Second Ignition	5 4 3 2 1
2.	Explanation of the development of the trademark for Holy Fire® III Karuna Reiki®	5 4 3 2 1
3.	Explanation of the registration process including manuals & certificates	5 4 3 2 1
4.	Third Ignition	5 4 3 2 1
5.	Practice using each Karuna I symbol with the Holy Fire® symbol w/partner(s)	5 4 3 2 1
6.	Explanation of how to conduct Experiences, Placements and Ignitions	5 4 3 2 1
7.	Explanation of how to practice Holy Fire® Meditation	5 4 3 2 1

Day 3:		5 – Excellent 1 - Poor
1.	Fourth Ignition	5 4 3 2 1
2.	Practice using each Karuna II symbol with the Holy Fire® symbol w/partner(s)	5 4 3 2 1
3.	Explanation & demonstration of chanting and toning; practice chanting w/partner(s). This can be done as part of step #2 using Holy Fire® or any of the other symbols.	5 4 3 2 1
4.	Discussion of teaching and class outlines	5 4 3 2 1
5.	Explanation of Healing Spirit Attachments	5 4 3 2 1

Holy Fire® and Karuna Reiki® are registered service marks of William Lee Rand.

Additional Comments:

Anatomy for Reiki

ILLUSTRATIONS BY TOM BOWMAN

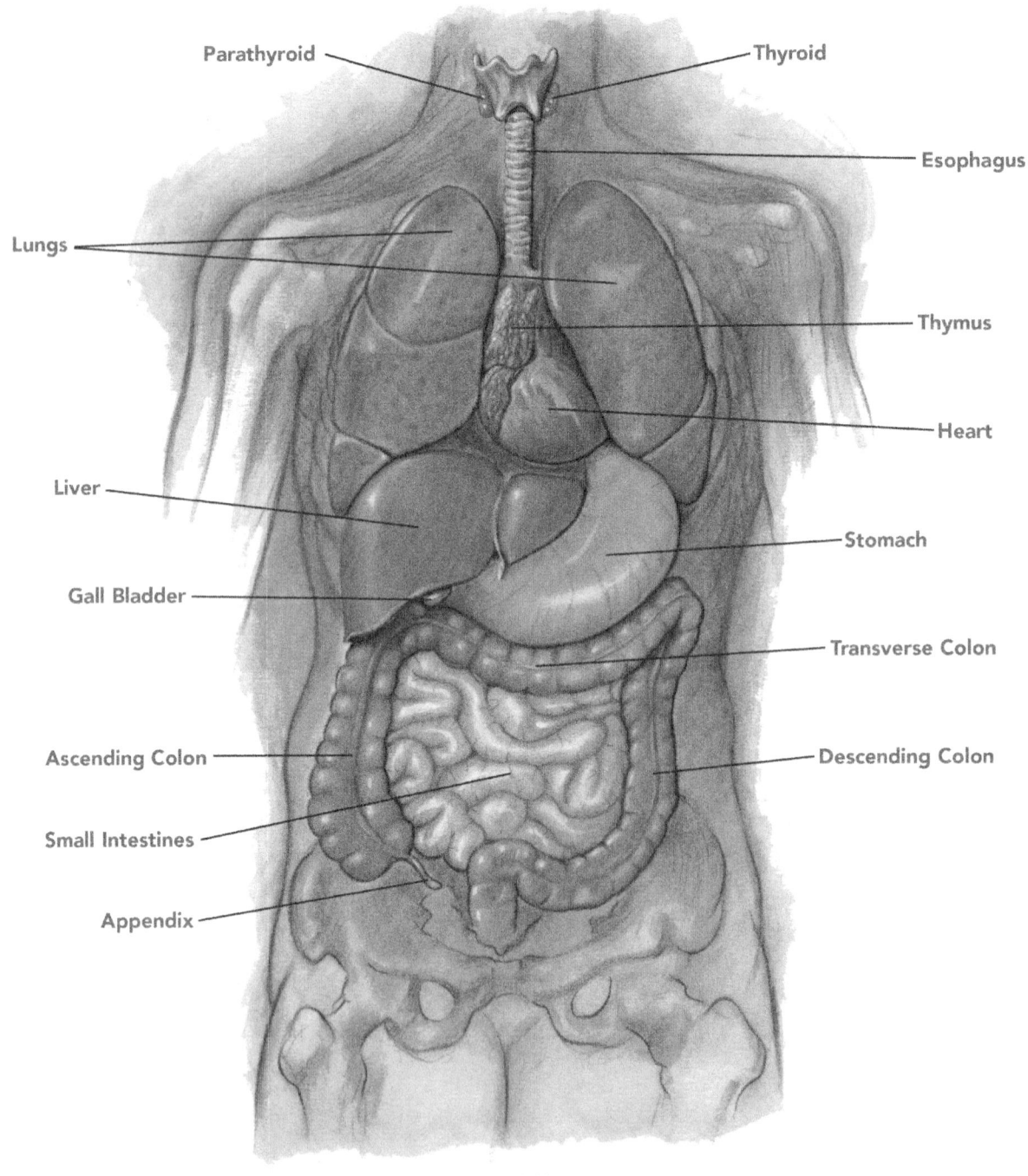

- Parathyroid
- Thyroid
- Esophagus
- Lungs
- Thymus
- Heart
- Liver
- Stomach
- Gall Bladder
- Transverse Colon
- Ascending Colon
- Descending Colon
- Small Intestines
- Appendix

Front View

© REIKI NEWS MAGAZINE

While an extensive understanding of anatomy is not necessary for Reiki practitioners, there are times when a basic knowledge of the major organs of the body is helpful, and even necessary. These include when the client has a condition or illness involving a specific organ(s) that needs treatment or when working in a clinic or hospital where communication with medical personnel about a client's condition is necessary.

Adrenals: Part of the endocrine system, the adrenals secrete hormones that regulate various functions in the body, one of which is the flight or fight response.

Appendix: The appendix is located at the beginning of the colon on the lower right side of the abdominal cavity. It is medically said to have no function.

Colon: Consisting of the ascending, transverse and descending sections, this tube-like organ is also called the large intestine and joins the small intestine on the lower right side of the abdominal cavity. The final processes of digestion take place in the colon with the absorption of water from fecal matter.

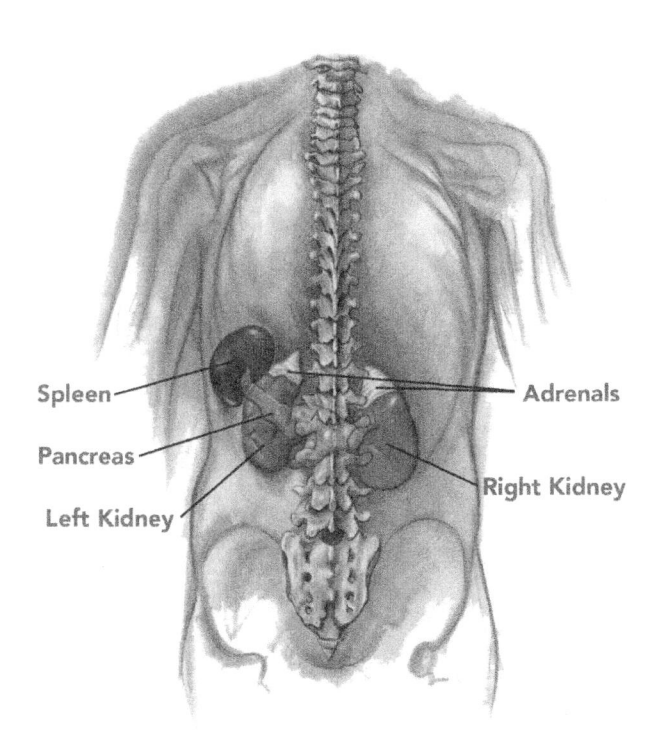

Heart: This is the muscular organ that pumps blood to all parts of the body. The rhythmic beating of the heart is a ceaseless activity, lasting from before birth to the end of life.

Kidneys: The purpose of the kidneys is to separate urea, mineral salts, toxins and other waste products from the blood, and to conserve water, salts and electrolytes.

Liver: The liver is the largest glandular organ of the body and has many functions including filtering debris and bacteria from the blood, converting excess carbohydrates and protein into fats and producing blood-clotting factors and vitamins A, D, K and B12. It also produces bile, which is used to prepare fats for digestion.

Lungs: The lungs are elastic organs used for breathing; they oxygenate the blood.

Pancreas: The pancreas is a glandular organ that secretes digestive enzymes and hormones. It also produces insulin, which lowers the blood-sugar level and increases the amount of glycogen (stored carbohydrate) in the liver.

Parathyroid: These four small glands are often embedded in the thyroid gland and govern calcium and phosphorus metabolism.

Small Intestine: Located between the stomach and colon, the small intestine digests and absorbs nutrients from food. This process is aided by secretions from the liver and pancreas.

Spleen: The spleen acts as a filter against foreign organisms that infect the bloodstream, and also filters out old red blood cells from the bloodstream and decomposes them.

Stomach: The stomach is the part of the digestive tract between the esophagus and the small intestine.

Back View

Esophagus: The esopagus is the portion of the digestive tube that moves food from the mouth to the stomach.

Gallbladder: Connected to the liver, the gallbladder stores and secretes bile, which aids digestion of fats.

Thymus: The thymus gland helps in the development and functioning of the immune system.

Thyroid: Part of the endocrine system, the thyroid gland secretes hormones necessary for growth and metabolism.

© REIKI NEWS MAGAZINE

The International Center For Reiki Training

The Center has been in operation since 1991. Our philosophy and purpose are listed on page 9. Our web site is at www.reiki.org and contains 1000 pages of Reiki information including over 400 articles on Reiki. Our Karuna web site is at www.karunareiki.org. We also offer a hard copy magazine and a free on-line newsletter. We are here to serve the Reiki community.

Purchasing Holy Fire® III Karuna Reiki® Manuals

Manuals for all the classes can be purchased directly from the Center - www.reikiwebstore.com.

The International Center for Reiki Training
21421 Hilltop St., #28, Southfield, MI 48033
Ph. 800-332-8112, 248-948-8112, Fax 248-948-9534
Web: www.reiki.org   Email: center@reiki.org

The Book On Karuna Reiki®

*Advanced Healing Energy
for Our Evolving World*

By Laurelle Shanti Gaia
Foreword by William Lee Rand

Karuna Reiki® is a healing energy that assists us in awakening to Universal compassion and the wisdom of our soul. Compassion is a state of consciousness, which when combined with energy, has great transformational power.

Karuna Reiki® has evolved as a result of a partnership, or co-creatorship between humanity and the Divine through the worldwide practice of Usui Reiki.

IN THIS BOOK YOU WILL LEARN ABOUT:

- The historical and spiritual origins of Karuna Reiki®
- Uses for the Karuna symbols
- Discerning spiritual guidance
- Using Karuna energy with crystals and gemstones
- Working with Archangel realms, spiritual masters, and Divine temples
- Visualization and prayer in healing; including sample prayers
- The evolving human subtle energy system
- Cellular and soul level healing
- Karuna techniques assist in healing or facilitating: Addictive Behavior, Allergies, Anxiety, Bleeding, Cellular Memory Release, Chakra Balancing, Chemotherapy, Delusion and Denial, Developing Healthy Habits, Ancestors and Future, Karmic Issues, Mental Focus and Grounding, Physical Injuries-Emergencies, Resistance to Healing, and Spiritual Growth
- How to give a Karuna session including, preparing sacred space, the healing altar, preparing the client
- Personal, physical preparations for spiritual work

Book Size 9 1/4 x 7 1/2 - Illustrated 160 pages

OP600   **$22.95 US**

There is a realm that blends Heaven and Earth, where Truth and Wisdom reside. In this realm we access our limitless potential as Divine beings.

This sacred place offers a wealth of spiritual knowledge, creative inspiration, blessings and guiding energies that assist our soul's progression.

Karuna Reiki® can help us experience this level of consciousness as a very special place of blending, co-creation and heightened spiritual awareness.

About the Author: *Laurelle Shanti Gaia is dedicated to creating and sharing opportunities for spiritual growth and healing through her writing, seminars, retreats and work with clients. For over 25 years she has studied and taught spiritual disciplines such as Reiki, Karuna Reiki®, color energy, yoga, and angelic communication. She is Director of Teacher Licensing for the ICRT, and facilitates healing retreats in the U.S. and worldwide.*

Karuna Reiki® is a registered trademark of the International Center for Reiki Training

Order From ICRT, Phone 1-248-948-8112, 800-332-8112 or from our web site at **www.reiki.org**